HOW TO
RAISE AN
INDEPENDENT
CHILD

HOW TO
RAISE AN
INDEPENDENT
CHILD

Shirley Gould

St. Martin's Press
New York

Library of Congress Cataloging in Publication Data

Gould, Shirley, 1917-
How to raise an independent child.

1. Children--Management. 2. Child psychology.
I.Title
HQ769.G718   649'.1   79-16794
ISBN 0-312-39610-4

To my parents
Rose and Abraham Goldman
Their memory is a blessing

Contents

HOW TO
RAISE AN
INDEPENDENT
CHILD

What is Independence?

We parents are required to perform two opposing tasks: to protect our children who are dependent on us, and simultaneously teach them to be independent, free of our control and competent to function independently. I do not refer to economic independence, although we certainly want that to come to them as adults, but rather to the kind of emotional independence that will enable them to live fully and freely.

Children cannot start life independently. They are dependent on others for a very long period of time, longer than any other mammal offspring. We must protect and nurture human beings from infancy throughout their dependence but do so in a way that helps them become independent adults.

Obviously we cannot treat them as helpless human beings if we want them to think of themselves as competent. We cannot prolong their submission and expect them to become autonomous. Yet, as we protect them, and take care of them, we want at the same time to teach them to be free of our control and competent to function independently. Our own misgivings may direct us to keep them under our control so that they do not fall under the control of any one else. We may mistake *hovering* for loving, and act as if they will stay connected to us forever, although we know they must be prepared for life apart from us. Sometimes we surround them with our love and concern in such a way that we actually fence them in.

Yet we know that we will not always be around to be their mentors. Under normal expectations they will outlive us by twenty years or more. Besides, the circumstances of contemporary life may require that our children be separated from one parent or another at various times during their childhood.

In our wiser moments we realize that the only way our children can cope even later with a world in constant change is to learn early to make their own decisions, to feel confident of their own abilities, and to function under their own initiative. We want them to be able to do what they have to even if no one is present to tell them what to do. In fact, we hope they will have the strength of character to resist the person or group that would tell them to do something in contradiction to the values we hold.

Various events of the last two decades have caused parents to wonder what they might have done when their children were small to help them build safeguards against the outside forces that led young adults into behavior that was often bizarre by existing standards or illegal under existing laws.

After children have grown up and left the family, it is too late to introduce corrective measures, but when they are young and still dependent, it is possible to help them to develop their individual sense of worth so that they are better able to resist damaging outside influences.

Earlier in this century, parents did not often face this particular kind of problem. When they did, it was in a rare instance. Families lived as their forebears had: parents raising children in the same way they had been raised. Children learned competence by observing others and by taking part in the family's struggle for survival. There were many more simple tasks that required the contribution of every family member. Children were expected to pitch in as soon as they were physically able. Their future independence was taken for granted. Everyone had to fend for himself. Because the birth of children was the automatic result of marriage, their upbringing was more likely to be taken for granted. They may have been considered burdens, but children were soon expected to become part of the family system, contributing their share to the life of the family and making their own way in the world at an early age. Even as young adults, they were expected to live in the family home and contribute to its support and upkeep until they left to start families of their own.

At the same time, those families were more likely to stay together. The usual development was for young people to mature, marry, and settle down near the rest of the family. There was thus a bulwark of support in the immediate vicinity for young families raising children, and this support was often used. Conditions of life did not change drastically from one generation to the next, and the elders of the family could and did provide advice and guidance to the younger members as needed. Sometimes that advice, though needed and requested, was not heeded, but there was comfort for all family members in knowing that it was available.

Even more valuable was the availability of other family

members for actual help. They could be summoned to assist in the physical acts of taking care of children, and usually they responded. They were accessible. Babysitting as an occupational title came into use fairly recently, because until the mobility brought on by World War II, families were much more likely to be clustered together and to take care of one another. There were maids and housekeepers for those who could afford to hire them, but there was no such job as "baby-sitter." Aunts and grandmothers did that.

Changes in society over the past several decades have disrupted this pattern, and it is highly unlikely it will ever be reestablished. Families are smaller and parents have less opportunity to consult their elders. Even when they do, the recommended activities, the patterns that worked before, are no longer applicable. Life conditions have changed so drastically that the responsibility of raising a child causes doubts and anxieties for many parents. In the zeal to provide for the welfare of children, we run the risk of unnecessarily prolonging the dependence of young people, thereby hampering their subsequent attempts to function in the world. One of the frustrations of parenthood is trying to decide when to protect a youngster and when to let the youngster discover a piece of the world all alone. We worry that the child will be injured or will suffer unexpected consequences of an action.

As we think of raising a child to be independent, we hardly know what independence is. The American Declaration of Independence in its whole text mentions the word "independence" only three times, and sheds no light at all on the subject of individual independence. Its purpose was merely to announce the intention of the separate states to be disconnected, that is independent, from Great Britain.

Certainly we do not want separation from our children when we think of them as independent people. We want to continue to be connected to them, but to treat them so that they will be able to function independently—without us—as need arises. One of the dictionary definitions for independence is "freedom from dependence" and another is "exemption from reliance on, or control by, others." There are two more that apply to people: "self-subsistence or maintenance" and "direction of one's own affairs without interference."

Clearly, in the context of parents raising children, we must have a more appropriate definition. Let us say that our objective in raising children is to help them to become sufficiently independent to cope with the challenges of life, to work and live in harmony with other people, and to enhance their own satisfactions in living.

To achieve that state, children must be helped *from earliest infancy* to function independently to the extent of their capacity. This means that as they grow and change their capacity increases, and their freedom to function must also increase. Throughout childhood and into adolescence they will swing from dependence to independence, sometimes to the consternation of their parents and other adults. The role of the adults is to foster the independence rather than the dependence, while providing for valid needs.

It isn't always possible to know when a request or demand for attention or service is valid, but an effective yardstick can be used. "Is this a reasonable request that the child cannot fulfill herself?" does not always have a clear answer, but at least asking the question helps to discover what is going on in the relationship between the child and the adult. An infant's demands are often inconvenient. It may be harder to separate such excesses from real needs in the case of infants, because they are so totally dependent upon us, but it is well to be aware that they can occur.

Parents falter very early because it's often so much fun to amuse an infant or a toddler. The reward of the first smiles is so great that a parent can fall into the habit of amusing a baby who can amuse himself. In so doing, we teach a child to be dependent on us rather than independent. We demonstrate the payoff for helplessness. Rather, we should be encouraging the growth of self-sufficiency.

Especially during the first year, a parent has to make new decisions almost continuously. Growth and development are so rapid that what you did last month or last week may no longer be appropriate. In order for such decisions to make sense, one must have a foundation of purpose on which to base one's judgments.

Thus, to help a baby gain confidence in herself and the world, an adult rushes to answer the first cry of the infant in the early weeks, but as the infant grows, she becomes more capable of tolerating delay. As early as three months old, the infant can wait ten minutes to be cared for if, for example, the adult is in the shower when the infant wakes.

There is a difference between the awakening cry and the fearful or anxious cries. As an infant grows, his repertoire of sounds increases and adults learn to distinguish them. The contented babble that begins in the last half of the first year is not the same as the stressful, piercing shrieks that require immediate attention. Only through observation and experience can the adult learn the appropriate response. The babble is the sound of a baby entertaining himself, and need not be answered nor interrupted.

Another kind of demand that a young child makes even before she has language is the sound often accompanied by a reaching gesture towards what you're eating or holding or to something on the table. Interpret this as a sign that the baby can now tell the difference between what she has and what someone else has. It is evidence of her growing intelligence and discernment. From the parent's perspective, it may be inconvenient, but from the baby's perspective, it's an opportunity to learn. If possible, let the baby have a taste, or touch, or look at the desired object. If it's food, it may help the infant to move toward eating what the rest of the family eats, eliminating the necessity for baby food. Each incident requires a specific decision, but the decision is to be based on the principle of increasing awareness and increasing independence for the child.

The child who is becoming independent is the one who very early, making an attempt to do something alone, is allowed to do so. Late in the first year, a baby usually learns to stand up in the crib. Wait for him to get up before you lift him out. Don't hand everything to an infant. As soon as she begins to be able to move about, let her go after the toy she wants rather than hand it to her. But don't move it away just to have the fun of watching her move; that leads to unnecessary frustration for the baby.

At each stage of growth, almost every day, a baby will attempt to do something new. Watch, encourage, and don't stifle the striving. The typical toddler in the third year of life begins to try to dress himself. He will put on his own shirt as soon as he can make an attempt, even if it goes on backward. He'll be proud that he could do it and won't care that it's backward unless an adult makes an issue of it. The next day and the day after that he'll learn to put it on properly, providing his first attempts haven't been thwarted. Parents don't need endless patience, just tolerance for error, a willingness to accept imperfection.

The child who is becoming independent has the privilege of privacy as she tries to push a truck across the floor, lost in a daydream of bigness. Her parent doesn't interrupt with a flow of questions. Her absorption in her task is the signal to save the conversation for another time.

The child who is learning to be independent can amuse himself, taking the responsibility for his own entertainment. He's a good companion, who won't interrupt what an adult is occupied with in order to force the adult to notice him. Children can be very demanding, but that doesn't mean that parents or other adults must respond to every demand. In order for a child to learn what is expected, the adult response must be tailored to the situation. For the development of mutual respect, the parent must respect the child's absorption in play and the child can learn to respect a parent's privacy. When the response of the parents is calm, brief, and detached from the child's demands, the child learns to limit those demands. In the absence of urgent needs such as a diaper change, preparation for rest, or mealtime, much of the annoying behavior of children is for the purpose of keeping parents busy with them, of gaining attention and service. When adults do not respond to such pressure, the annoying behavior abates.

The independent school girl remembers to take her books and equipment to school without constant reminders, and later remembers her homework. She brings it home and attends to it without the interrogation of anyone else.

As a child grows in independence, he or she makes a growing contribution to the well-being of the family as a whole and learns cooperation with other family members and persons outside the family. Such a child learns to give as well as to receive, to operate autonomously as well as in the group.

Naturally children vary in their rate of development, and what one child can do at age three another may not master until age four, or may have already accomplished at age two. Each child is an individual, and must be observed as such, even though the charts of development can, in a general way, be very helpful. Within the same family, sisters and brothers, even twins, may not operate on the same timetable. Only the person who is in a direct close relationship with a child can estimate the youngster's level of competence, but the relationship between the child and others is an ongoing force. Thus, it is of greater value to emphasize the interaction between the child and others than to memorize the developmental stages. It is the interaction between the infant and other people that largely determines how the young one's ideas and behavior will develop. In general, children are capable of much more than we give them credit for, at any time. We need to let them try and not berate them if they fail. Mistakes are the proof of effort as effort is the fuel for action.

chapter two

Why are Children Dependent?

To begin to learn to help our children become independent let us first consider the difference between human children and other animal offspring, similar to us but very different. We, that is, humankind, belong to the class of living beings that are called "mammals." All of us mammals, human and animal, have backbones and skin at least partially covered with hair. The young are suckled. One of the subdivisions among mammals is the species called "primates." That's the one we belong to, along with other creatures who share some of our characteristics.

We are of course distinctive in many ways, especially in the size of our brains, enabling us to think and to reason, and in our ability to walk upright and to grasp objects with thumb and fingers.

Raising a human child is an exceedingly complex task, especially compared to animal parenting. Animals breed, bear, and raise their young by instinct, and adapt their habits according to the environment in which they happen to live. We can assume that they don't worry about whether they're doing it right, for there is a limited number of ways they can function. If they are in the wild, survival is the most urgent goal, and if they are confined either in a zoo or domestically, they are limited by the conditions around them.

Animal young need only to be trained for survival, that is, to get food and shelter when they leave their parents. The education they need is completed at an early age.

Human young, however, need the care of adults for a longer period than the young of any other mammal. The complex of skills needed to take one's place in the world requires language, learning and decision-making far beyond what is necessary for survival of other species. These skills are developed from mental and emotional capabilities, but simultaneously, the human infant has a long course of physical development. This, too, is much slower in humans than in other mammals.

Animals are usually fully grown and independent of the mother at the time they are weaned, which varies. Dogs are suckled for about six weeks and reach maturity in one to two years, while most species of cat reach puberty in twelve to fifteen months. Gorillas are largely or completely independent of their mothers some time between age three and age six. Some monkeys reach puberty in three or four years. Although puberty is usually considered to be equivalent with full growth, Indian elephants reach sexual maturity some time between their eighth and twelfth year, and physical growth may continue to age twenty-five. That sounds something like a human's rate.

We who live in civilization don't have much opportunity to watch the development of our fellow creatures, especially such as elephants and gorillas, but we do see some of them. In a museum, I have watched through the glass as a fertile egg cracks and a newly hatched chick breaks out. In only a few minutes, such a chick opens its eyes and can walk away. Hamsters and gerbils reproduce rapidly, crowding the cages we provide for them and raising their young quickly to independence. How easy for those parents!

Contrast such instinctive behavior, such rapid growth, with the development rate in the life of a human infant, who has so far to go, and so long to grow. Nearly thirty per cent of the entire life span of a baby will be spent in physical and mental growth, and even long after physical growth is completed, mental and emotional growth goes on. That's what distinguishes "man" as a learning rather than a purely instinctive being. Each human has to learn to behave rather than just act on instinct, because we live in a society with a specific culture, codes of behavior, standards, and values.

Man is also a social being. That is, we people live among others of our kind, and depend upon one another for the very maintenance of life. We speak and interact, and our well-being depends not only on our own efforts, but on our cooperation or competition with others. We live in a set of relationships with other people. Those relationships vary from the most intimate, as in the family, to the most remote, as in people we watch on television who influence our choices and activities.

Keeping in mind the rapid physical growth of other animals, consider the human baby. At four months the infant cannot usually sit up alone, much less stand, still needs to suckle from breast or bottle, and is only beginning to eat from a spoon as our culture requires. That is, while an animal bites food directly with teeth, people are expected to use spoons and forks to transport food to the mouth. In some cases it is permissible to pick up food in the hands—a hot dog or a piece of pizza, for instance, but not often do we lower our heads to attack food directly with our teeth and lips.

Language, essential to the communication with others, doesn't begin until a child is about a year old. That's also the time that a human can begin to move about freely, either on feet or hands and knees.

By the age of three a youngster is usually trained to use the toilet, another artifact of civilization. Such a child can probably feed himself, begin to dress himself, and maneuver stairs. Clothing and staircases are also of distinctly human manufacture. At this age a child often begins a regular school program, but it will be many years before the pupil has sufficient education to function as an adult in a technologically advanced society such as ours.

In the first few years education is mainly the responsibility of parents, but by the age of six, formal schooling begins according to law. Public education in the U.S. is regulated separately by each of the fifty states, but school attendance is compulsory at least until a child becomes sixteen years old. Only Mississippi has no compulsory attendance law. The advances of technology make it desirable for most students to be in school past the age of sixteen in order to acquire enough education. Persons who cannot read or write, whether they have been in school or not, find it hard to support themselves in our society for there are hardly any jobs left for unskilled laborers. Twelve years of public education is now considered a minimum requirement for most jobs.

Beyond the minimum, to qualify for more sophisticated occupations, additional years of education are required. This may continue for as long as ten to fifteen additional years often requiring financial support from parents long after their offspring have reached physical and sexual maturity.

Thus has society made it more complicated for a young person to become independent and for parents to foster independence. In simpler times, young people could be out on their own while still in their teens and manage to survive by doing whatever work was available. Now we have the contradicting situation in which parents continue to give support while at the same time their absolute rule is no longer valid. The same changes in our culture that made longer dependency necessary have made autocratic rule impossible.

For decades we parents assumed that we could get by raising our children by chance and by instinct, but we now realize that such efforts don't always produce the desired results.

There are two ways of considering a child as independent. One is more appropriately termed the neglected child: the one who is left to fend for himself or herself and manages to survive alone, sometimes with the help of outsiders, sometimes purely by his or her own wits and efforts. The other is the child who gradually becomes independent while continuing to enjoy the necessary dependence on parents and family. This way will be the focus of this book.

In the mid-nineteenth century, many children were forced to be independent. Among them were many homeless boys, especially in the cities. Often poor people who were parents could not support themselves or their children. Sometimes rampant disease meant early death for fathers and mothers. Orphan children without care or shelter were out on the streets, selling papers, begging, scavenging, and doing whatever they could just to stay alive. They were independent, but not in a way we would want for our children today.

The plight of such children led to the concept of the "dependent child" and the development of social agencies and systems to cope with their condition. Orphan asylums were created. With all their faults they did rescue children from total neglect. One of the other intriguing efforts to save them was the "mission to children" undertaken by Charles Loring Brace in New York City. In a time when there was no compulsory school attendance or laws against hiring children for labor, the efforts of the Children's Aid Society he founded were to find "paying work" locally for some and to move others into the country to homes where they could earn their keep by working. For some children, this was really an improvement; for others, it was to exchange one kind of misery for another, far removed from any familiar places or faces. While some of the children were virtually adopted into new families and treated well, others were not much more than slaves or indentured servants.

Not only were individual children placed in homes, but large groups were taken as far west as Illinois and Michigan. One trip in 1854 took sixty-six boys and seventy-two girls to be distributed among families in Pennsylvania. They were accepted by farmers and other employers who would feed, clothe, and shelter them in return for their labor. Remember that a very large number of families farmed land without machinery at that time, and more hands were always welcome.

Such movements of children continued until about 1930, supported by church groups and others who wanted to help meet the needs of children who were considered, lacking parents, to be dependent on the public.

From such well-intentioned efforts grew the system of child welfare that exists today. Child labor laws came early in this century through the efforts of crusaders like Jane Addams, who like Brace wanted to help the poor and helpless. As time went on and especially after World War II, the needs and rights of children received extra emphasis.

Partly as the result of the absence of thousands of adult males from their homes and normal occupations during World War II, the post-war thrust was toward family life. The word "togetherness" was coined as a promotional device for a woman's magazine, but it came into common use because it fit the mood of the country. Young women, who had postponed marriage and child-bearing because of the absence of so many men, gave up their wartime jobs and activities to become housewives, to bear and raise children, and to give family life top priority.

Other changes were also taking place. Men who had never been away from home had seen the rest of the world and found some of it attractive. Industries, greatly expanded to meet the needs of a wartime economy, transferred employees from one end of the country to the other and their families went too. Advances in transportation and communication caused many young couples to settle far away from their original surroundings and from their older relatives.

The nuclear family—father, mother, and child or children—was planted and grew in a new neighborhood without the old ties, and without the support that might have been available. It was often begun in suburbia, on land that had so recently been farmland that carrots would still sprout in the ground seeded for grass. Schools, churches, governments, and community activities had to be created by the very people who needed them.

Young parents of the post-World War II period, particularly mothers, concentrated their best efforts on their homes and especially their children. Removed from the influences of their own childhood, they wanted to protect their young from the stress they had survived. Some of them were children of the Great Depression and knew real deprivation. They didn't want their children to suffer so. As a result, these youngsters were watched over, catered to, chauffeured, lessoned, and indulged in the belief that this would help them have better lives, however "better" was defined by their parents. Expressed in language, parents often said, "I want my children to have everything I didn't have."

Over-emphasis on their children did not, however, produce the desired results, either for parents or their young. Instead, in the opinion of many, such treatment produced a generation selfish but not self-sufficient, rebellious but not productive, and in any case determined to shape their own adult lives differently. Parents, especially mothers, reflected on the years they devoted to their children and wondered why they did not feel satisfied with the outcome.

Now that such extremes of childrearing are no longer idealized, and parents have a more realistic view of family life, it is hard to know how to perform as a parent. Clearly, the very old rule of authority in which the man of the house has the most authority, the woman next, and the children do what they're told, has expired. Some adults may still believe in it, but they soon discover that it doesn't work.

Neither can we return to the child-centered times when

children came first and were to be indulged in their every whim. Some call this the permissive period, meaning that anything a child wanted, or wanted to do, was permissible. We realize now that each member of the family has rights as well as needs, and the only way to achieve that for everyone is through a system of cooperation in which each family member contributes to the well-being of all.

In order for such a system to operate, each child has to become as capable as possible as early as possible. Becoming independent about his or her own person and activities to the limit of his or her capacity leaves room and time for making a contribution to the family group. Feeling independent to the extent of one's capability also makes it less likely that a child will sabotage the efforts of others. The child who feels independent in some aspects of his or her life is the child whose self-esteem is growing. Such a youngster is an asset to family harmony.

Those of us raising children in families do not wish to cast our children out into the world before they are ready. Our aim instead is to prepare them day-by-day for the independence they can handle so that as they reach maturity they can also reach individual independence. This is much to be preferred over the kind of independence that characterizes the neglected child.

chapter three

Why do We Want Our Children to Become Independent?

In a corner of every parent's mind is the dream picture of adult offspring, fully grown, operating autonomously, and bringing credit and honor to the parents who helped them reach that point. We think of our little ones as we hope they will be in a decade or two and focus all our own fantasies on them. Depending on our own shortcomings, we see them having everything we lack: tall if we're short, beautiful (or handsome) if we're plain, successful in work and love and friendship. We want them to finish what we started and also reach complete fulfillment in their own lives.

As we look around, however, we see that children as they grow up don't fit that picture. They are not all well prepared for adult life. We can recall times in our own lives when we ourselves have not functioned well. Sometimes we long for the privilege of crawling up on somebody's lap, perhaps to suck a thumb. We want to be comforted and have our problems solved. One of the hardest things to accept when we lose a parent is the fact that we have no one to turn to any more—even if we weren't able to depend on that parent. As each of us carries within us such feelings of childhood, we know that our children will also carry into adult life some childish traits.

When our children are small, it is a source of joy and satisfaction that they need us so much. This is true even as we chafe at the burden they bring us. We like being the powerful people to whom they turn. But none of us knows where we will be tomorrow, let alone years from now, and we certainly can't predict how much we will be able to help our children when they get older. As they celebrate each succeeding birthday and move through each grade in school, we become increasingly aware that they will have to function alone and without us some time in the future.

This is no different than it has been for generations. What is different is the rapid change in our society and in the environment in which we live. Nothing is constant except human strivings and needs, and even those must adapt to the times. The world we know is in an almost continuous state of change, some of it for better. Some of it seems to be for worse. But as it happens, we have very little power to affect it; it is we who are affected by it. Just as we became accustomed to the machinery of technology that brought us the automobile, the automatic washing machine, and the vacuum cleaner, we were confronted with scientific developments that brought us the television receiver followed closely by the computer. Nor can we forget about splitting the atom—making nuclear destruction possible, together with its peaceful counterpart, nuclear energy.

Even so, many of the devices that govern our daily lives

are not machines in the traditional sense. We accepted the new machinery eagerly: the telephone, the electric light, the airplane. But the newest inventions are not collections of moving parts designed to do work that we humans would otherwise perform. The television and the computer don't do that kind of visible work. Instead, they have changed the ways we communicate and, more important, the speed of all kinds of communication. The fact that we live in a society that is so connected to the processes of technology emphasizes for us the reality of human life and the necessity of social living. Carrying this principle into the family, it helps us to realize that our children need to learn to function as thinking, feeling human beings in a society otherwise dominated by science and technology and their devices.

It also reminds us that just as we have been forced to accommodate ourselves to change during our lifetimes there is no way to predict what additional developments will face our children as they assume their adult lives. There is no sign that change is diminishing. Instead, there are abundant signs that the rate of change is increasing.

Alfred Kadushin, one of the foremost American authorities on the well-being of children, in his basic book, *Child Welfare Services* (New York: Macmillan, 1967) says:

> In a tradition-oriented society, the past is revered, and its custodians—parents and grandparents—are respected. In a society oriented toward change the orientation is toward the future, and the future is represented by the child.

This explanation may account for the excessive emphasis on the child mentioned earlier, but it is certainly true that we are undergoing massive and continuous change with which we must cope. Therefore we realize that we must direct our efforts toward preparing our children for the ever accelerating variations that are continually evolving, and will continue to assault them.

The only way we can help them to prepare for an unknown future is to help them now to learn to function independently and also in cooperation with other members of society. The ability to cope independently, which leads to feelings of self-confidence, is the asset that helps a person deal with whatever life presents. The child who grows up knowing how to master the problems of everyday living can best handle the onslaughts of change that the future may bring.

As we consider all those shifts in the way we live, we notice that the shape of family life is undergoing alteration too. We look around at our neighbors, friends, and relatives and see the disruption wrought either by divorce or by changes in the roles of parents. More mothers are working through necessity or preference; more fathers are becoming active parents. We know vaguely that this is not confined to our own circles of acquaintances, and we are not immune to the effects. Even when we feel that our own family life is stable and secure, we become annoyed that we must accept drastic disruptions in the lives of families around us. That annoyance often arises from our inner feeling that we may also be subjected to disruption in our own household. While we hope for the continuation of our current relationships, we are compelled to notice that we are also subject to the strains and tensions that contribute to breakups among others.

The U. S. Bureau of the Census confirms our impressions in its scholarly reports and tells us how widespread is the phenomenon of change. In its 1974 publication that covers trends and prospects for the last half of the twentieth century, it tell us:

> The proportion of men and women who were divorced and had not remarried by the survey date increased considerably between 1950 and 1970, with most of the increase occurring in the 1960s, when divorce rates went up sharply.

If we had any doubts, they are thus dispelled. More and more people are getting divorced, and more and more people who once expected to live happily married ever after find themselves facing long periods of being unmarried and alone. Many of them are parents, with and without custody of children. Each of us faces such a possibility, not only through divorce but through the possibility of death. It is not a pleasant prospect.

The Cenus report goes on to say that most people who are divorced do remarry, some quite soon, and some after a few years:

> The data discussed here seem to demonstrate that a fundamental modification of life styles and values relating to marriage has been taking place during the last two decades.

Most of this is obvious to us as we look around, but it is confirmed by the actual counting of individuals performed by the U. S. Census and by the interpretations of the Census experts. Their stated projection is:

> Estimates indicate that, among persons about thirty years old at present, close to ninety-five percent have married or will eventually marry, close to one-third will obtain a divorce, and close to four out of every five of those who obtain a divorce will eventually remarry.

These comments about marriage do not mention the children of those marriages, but we know that children are bound to be affected. No matter how carefully a mother and father break a marriage and how intelligent they are about informing their child or children, having divorced parents cannot be the same as having two parents who are together. Even the new fashion for shared custody does not cancel the harmful effects of seeing one's parents split. This is even disregarding the many divorces that occur under bitter, hostile and spiteful conditions.

This particular report also points out that we in the United States have a higher rate of geographical mobility than any other country, and that most of this moving has happened since the end of World War II. Moving around may be beneficial to an adult's career, and thus bring about improved living conditions for families, but it is certainly a strain on everyone involved. Children who are learning their way in the world are transported to what is in many ways a new world, and have only their own skills and personalities to help them make connections all over again.

Those children who are on the way to independent functioning are best prepared to make new friendships and thus to fit into a new community.

Pointing up the changes that children might have to contend with should not, however, let us lose sight of the fact that six out of every seven families in the United States were still maintained by a married couple in 1970. The news isn't all bad. Assuming that yours is one of the stable families, raising children with two parents in a place where you've been living for a few years, you still can have no guarantee that your lives will continue to progress at the steady pace that would allow you to supervise your children's daily activities indefinitely and to be always available when they need you.

We have been thinking about all the influences of the world on the individual, and how they are constantly changing. But there is another aspect of life that calls for independence, and that is the outlook of a person, the result of the feelings within. Dr. Martin Seligman, author of *Helplessness* (San Francisco: Freeman, 1975) has been studying the connection between helplessness and depression for many years. He concludes that a feeling of helplessness and the onset of depression are bound together and offers ample evidence that this is so.

Dr. Seligman says that the helpless person becomes depressed in the belief that he or she is powerless to control what goes on outside the self. The inability to control either events or the elements of life that bring gratification, relieve suffering or provide nurture to a person is what leads to feelings of depression. Certainly none of us has the actual power to control events or to manipulate the elements of life that bring us joy. The difference between a depressed person and the rest of us is that we don't remind ourselves of our powerlessness. We're busy coping with what we can control; that is, doing our work in the world, and doing our best to relate to other people.

Depression usually breeds inactivity, which then contributes to the depressed feelings, closing the circle. One of the effective antidotes to depression is purposeful activity, and in fact, psychotherapists often prescribe just such activity to break the circle of low feelings.

Relating the connection between helplessness and depression to the child who must constantly turn to someone else for assistance, it is clear that one of the real dangers for such a child is that the inability to fend for herself or himself leads to a feeling of helplessness which may then lead to depression. This is hardly what we want for our children.

A depressed child finds life especially difficult. It is hard to venture out from home, make a friend, go to school, or find any success. Feelings of depression lead to continual discouragement, verifying the feelings of helplessness and causing great concern to parents and teachers.

The child who has feelings of self-confidence and knows that she or he can do what is necessary in the conduct of daily life is much less likely to succumb to feelings of depression and/or helplessness. This is the child who has learned to be as independent as possible as often as possible; whose parents have set an example, taught what is necessary, and then constantly allowed the child to expand his or her abilities.

chapter four

When Can Independence Begin?

As we have all tried to learn to understand our children in the last few decades, we may have paid too much attention to timetables. We try to schedule our children's lives carefully so they will fit into prescribed stages. Then we worry if they don't make the passage from one stage to another at the designated time. One of the questions most often asked of me and of other family counselors is: "When can we start?" together with "Isn't it too late for that?", "Aren't they too young?" or "Aren't they too big?" Parents are afraid to do anything in relation to children at the wrong time, because it might harm rather than help their development.

Some of that fear may be justified, but it has to be tempered with common sense. The best answer to "When can independence begin?" is "Right now!" Of course I don't mean complete independence, but at any time in the life of your child, you can begin to make room for a measure of independence. If the child isn't quite ready to do what you have in mind, you can go back and try again later.

Some of the confusion about timetables and stages of

development comes from the simplification of scholarly works for public consumption. Certain key words from the work of experts seep into everyday language. One such is the word "immature." It is often loosely used to explain behavior we don't like in our children, or responses from them that are unexpected. Instead of doing anything about it, parents excuse such activity by calling it "immature," but then worry about it, and such worry stifles common sense.

Parents aren't sure exactly what the experts mean by "immaturity" and so they become overly cautious, or even neglectful. To have a handy label also means we can ignore the evidence for corrective action. We call the child, or the behavior, immature, and then sit back and wait for the child to outgrow it. As time goes by, and the behavior continues, a parent is likely to say, "Well, he's always been immature." Meanwhile, the child has received no encouragement to act in a more acceptable fashion, and the parent has lost some good opportunities to intervene.

The word "immature" is appropriate when it is used to describe the physical and biological processes of growth. The bones, muscles, and nerves of a newborn baby are certainly immature, and remain thus throughout the process of development. We can understand that. There's a lot of growing to come, and it will naturally ensue if the baby gets good nutrition, avoids disease and has healthful living conditions. We need only be concerned if normal growth appears to stop or be interrupted.

But with mental and emotional development, the word "immature" has been so overused that sometimes it just disguises ignorance. We see behavior we don't like and we call it "immature." Whenever a child does something of which we disapprove, acts in a way we dislike, or fails to conform to our expectations, we are apt to label the child "immature." Similarly, when a child uses language in the way that used to be called "fresh," we call it "immature."

What the word actually means is "not arrived at full development." It is precisely descriptive when it is applied to animals or plants. The puppy is immature until it grows into a dog. A budding ear of corn in the field or a maple sapling in the yard are both immature. With time, good weather, and perhaps some fertilizer both will eventually arrive at full development.

But for children, full development requires more. It requires interaction with the humans in the social system. Youngsters as they grow are affected by the language and actions of everyone with whom they come in contact. Not only time and good health facilitate their mental and emotional development, but the experiences they have with other people from their first days go into the system through which they develop their personalities and their emotional repertoire.

Without the continuous contact with persons, the human infant cannot learn to function in society. The human attribute that especially distinguishes us from animals is our use of language. In order to speak and understand, a baby must be spoken to. Language is only one example of a human trait a child must learn from others. By observing the reactions of the people around him or her, every infant forms ideas about what his or her own behavior ought to be.

Biological development follows a course which can be charted in a general way, but emotional development is much less predictable. We do know a lot about what kind of experiences a child needs in order to produce the behavior we like to call "mature," but no one child has the best conditions all the time. Even the best educated, best informed parents are fallible and nobody can control the whole environment.

Children do not, I repeat, follow precise timetables. Studies of large numbers of children and our own observation of others tell us approximately when an infant will sit up alone, stand, creep, and walk. But all we need to know is that the stages of development follow one another. It's a truism that a child has to stand before she can walk, and crawl before walking. But some babies skip crawling altogether. They didn't read the timetables. The inner mechanisms determine when each step is taken, and there's not much we can do about them. The prediction schedules can't tell us accurately in advance when any one child will sit up alone, show a tooth, or pull up to a standing position, but they do tell us in general terms what the stages are and how each one leads to another. That's part of what makes parenthood fun—watching the child grow and marveling at each new accomplishment.

Growth comes in small steps, sometimes so small as to seem that it has stopped for a while. At other times we see giant leaps, almost as though a child had taken a rest in order to put forth a spurt of energy.

There are also times when we see backsliding, sometimes called regression. This may happen as a result of illness, disruption in the usual schedule, or more likely a change in the family. The birth of a sibling typically evokes behavior that appears babyish. Moving to a new home, loss of a parent or close relative through divorce or death, or tension in the household caused by something the child doesn't understand are among the precipitating events for such behavior. In such situations, the role of the parent is to act as if you know that the child will recover from this episode and resume normal development. Consider this behavior as an interruption in development, and treat it as such. It may be difficult to give the extra attention and warmth that the child craves. But you don't need to feel guilty about your role in the disruption or your inability to do everything the child wants from you. Do what you can; accept the child's right to be upset; maintain your confidence in her or him that when this crisis is over the previous level of behavior will be recaptured.

When we forget about the differences in development among children, one of the errors we make as parents is to compare our child to others—to siblings, to other members of our families, or to the children of friends or neighbors. Sometimes we read the child development books and measure our own children by the graphs and charts we find in them. When we do this, we are judging ourselves as parents and also measuring our children. We hold up some arbitrary standard and feel that we and they have failed if they fall short.

In encouraging independence, we are most concerned with emotional development, although physical maturity must also be considered. The attitude of independence grows inside a person, tied to a feeling of confidence in one's self, in one's ability to cope. This has also been called a sense of mastery, and is related to competence in performing tasks. A feeling of independence is hard to imagine if it is not based on competence, for the person who is not competent must by definition depend on others. One of the hazards of an actual handicap is the feeling it produces of needing the help of others, thus robbing the handicapped person of complete independence.

A task that confronts a toddler is to open a door. Until Rachel could walk, she paid little attention to doors. Now that she can move around unaided, she notices them. She reaches for the door handle, and may not be tall enough. Depending on the individual rate of growth and on the height of the handle, a child may reach this sometime between the ages of two and four. Then she has to have the developed muscular ability in her hand to turn the knob, or press the handle down, or do whatever else is required before the door will open.

Whether you wish to allow her to open the door, or to encourage her, or even to help her, also depends on where the door leads. If it leads to the outside and then directly to the street, you probably do not want her to open the door and go out alone. If, however, it is the door to the bathroom where the potty is kept, it is a display of independence and a significant step toward maturity for Rachel to be able to open the door and use the potty.

As you observe your own child, you watch his efforts. If you have decided that independence is appropriate, you demonstrate how to open the door. Then you wait while he tries again. It may take only one demonstration, or it may take several attempts. You commend the effort, because you want to encourage the child to make it again. Be careful not to overemphasize your pleasure in the final achievement, because you don't want to convey the message that this is some kind of culmination. Rather, your message is: "I knew you could do it. That's fine."

If, however, independence is not appropriate (for instance, because the door leads to the street) you lead the child away from the door toward a different activity. You may also explain that danger lies beyond the door, but don't overemphasize that either, for the time will come to teach the child to go out through that door.

The answer, then, to the question "When can independence begin?" is that it can begin soon after birth, but the degree of independence any child can attain at any time is attached to the child's condition and the setting in which he or she functions.

No matter what age your child is as you read this, there is likely to be some area of his or her life in which you can foster greater independence. Generally this means that you or the other adult who is in closest contact with the child has to allow the child to do something himself or herself that someone else has been doing. Don't do anything for a child at almost any time that the child can do. For instance, you don't feed a child who can feed himself, nor do you dress and undress a child who can do it for herself. The difficulty is you have to discover just what the child can do, and in order to make that discovery you must refrain from doing it for him or her. If you do it, the child doesn't get a chance. This applies from earliest infancy and requires from the adult restraint coupled with caring, for it may be necessary, when the child cannot do what he or she set out to do, for the parent to finish the job. If the child is to try again, the adult's role must be a friendly not a punitive one. Accept the child's limitations of the moment and assume that next time will be more successful.

With a new skill, the child may falter from fatigue. In the latter half of the first year, a baby can begin to pick up food with his fingers and put it in his mouth. You encourage him to do so by putting a small quantity on the feeding tray, replenishing it when it is eaten. But when you see that it is beginning to be difficult for him and you notice that he is tired, you might want to feed him with a spoon. If a child is ill, you may give more help than usual. This applies as well to an older child: new tasks are best learned in small segments. Anyone who is overwhelmed by the magnitude of a job to be done is apt to get discouraged. The younger the child, the more susceptible he or she is. What a parent must avoid is making excuses to serve the child often. There will be times when you can't wait for the child to do it herself. Occasionally, then, you do it. But saying "hurry up" won't help. That only puts you in a contest with the child, with the possibility that as you say "hurry up" the child actually slows down.

As a general rule, watch what the youngster of any age can do, teach new skills as soon as you can and refrain from taking over. Even as you are teaching the child is learning and needs to practice in order for the learning to be complete. Be prepared to tolerate mess, for the child beginning to learn a new skill cannot be neat. Milk may spill, food may fall, other things may be scattered. Schedules may also be disrupted.

If your child can talk, you have probably already heard, "Me do it myself!" It's one of the first sentences that toddlers utter, and it often starts a war because it takes longer for the little one to do what Mother can do in a moment. Or Father, or whoever is accustomed to caring for the child. This kind of conflict can continue throughout childhood and adolescence. It crops up whenever a youngster wants to do something that a parent can do better. Adults, having had more practice, want things done just right, but children aren't that fussy. They just want them done. If the children are going to learn competence and independence, they need constant practice in doing things for themselves.

Many opportunities for contributing to a child's independence are lost because we don't take the time. We live by the clock, and we're always in a hurry. A generation or two ago, people were much more subject to the vagaries of outside conditions—the weather, for instance. It controlled; Monday was wash day, but if it was raining hard, clothes couldn't be hung outside on the line, so the laundry was to wait until Tuesday, or even Wednesday. As long as the family had some clean clothes to wear, it didn't matter much. About the only thing on time was Sunday dinner. Despite the established routines that told women to wash on Monday, iron on Tuesday, dust on Wednesday and wash windows on Thursday, things got done when there was time and opportunity to do them. Shopping for food had to be done every day, but if there was a long wait until the butcher got the meat ready, the time was spent visiting with other customers, "passing the time of day."

Today, if the automatic washing machine breaks down, it's a major crisis, for we are programmed to do the wash quickly, at a specified allotted time.

But children don't operate on clock time. They go at their own pace, slowly sometimes, more quickly at others, according to their own inner works. When we attempt to interfere, telling them "hurry up" we defeat our own purposes, and destroy their beginning independence.

Our children must learn to function within the demands of the family schedules, but at a time of training there has to be enough leeway for them to learn the individual tasks that lead to independence and cooperation. Trying to hurry them may make it take longer. It's better to let a child set the pace, for without interruption and reminders she or he can concentrate better on the task.

It's never too soon. Dr. T. Berry Brazelton, pediatrician and author, expert on the newborn, has said, "We know that taste and touch probably begin while the baby is in the uterus. Smell comes shortly after birth. Hearing may also begin immediately."* Although the infant seems completely helpless, there are areas in which independence can be supported. Within a few weeks of birth, as the biological systems settle down, an infant cries in hunger, stops crying when fed, and stops nursing when full. Not long afterward, the baby begins to focus its sight, to raise its head, and can amuse herself or himself during the short waking periods.

To support this burgeoning independence, watch for the baby's signs of it, and don't interfere. Many a well-meaning parent has begun the process of thwarting a child by picking up the baby to show it off, or interrupting the baby's own attempts at amusing himself by entertaining him unnecessarily.

The newborn does not present a "clean slate," but comes into the world with individual uniqueness. Each infant is different. This can be readily seen in any hospital nursery. Yours, and every other infant, has specific inborn qualities and the way to bring out the best is to observe carefully and relate to the child you have, not the one you wished for, or the one you read about. If the one you have is in fact the one you wished for, you're already ahead. In your interaction with the infant, and later the child, you will have a tremendous influence on the kind of personality that emerges, but the infant is not just a

*March, 1978 meeting of the first International Conference on Child Studies, sponsored by Brown University, reported by "Focus on Children and Youth" Vol. V, No. 4, April, 1978, p. 16.

collection of cells; she or he is already a specific individual, like no other.

The response your child makes, and the behavior your baby produces, will be unique, even though the pattern of development will follow the generally expected stages. A person is not a machine, and one sibling is not just like another. The specific youngster with whom you are concerned will grow into a specific individual and your relationship with him or her will greatly influence the character of that person.

As the child grows older, your interaction is with a person who has already formed ideas about herself or himself, about life, and about the rest of the world. The child has also created a pattern of beliefs about the consequences of relationships with other people and acts on those beliefs.

But it isn't too late to enhance independence in the older child. You just have to watch where the child is and operate from that point. You try to assess her capabilities at the moment, not ahead, not behind, but right where she is. Your strategies toward independence depend on the qualities already evident.

At the later end of childhood, if you are thinking about an adolescent son or daughter who seems so dependent, you can quit some of the service you render in order to help a teenager become more independent. You might even have to cut down your nurture to young adult offspring, for nobody becomes independent when dependence is more attractive.

People can grow throughout life, as many have discovered. There's even a name for a whole new perception of what it is to be an adult. It's called the "Human Potential Movement" and includes an array of psychologies of behavior, all demonstrating that an adult no more than a child need not stop growing, even when physical growth is complete. Many adults have become able to throw off the constraints they carried with them into adult life to become more fully functioning human beings, more contented with themselves and with life. So it's never too late.

There is no particular stage in a child's life when independence can begin. It can start shortly after birth, or at any time thereafter. We do *not* wish to push on our children the kind of independence described in Chapter 2, through which a child is left without the support of adults to fend for himself. What we seek is the kind of independence that develops within the family with adequate support by adults when independence is not reached. Such support helps the child to make renewed efforts toward ultimate autonomy.

chapter five

The Paradox of Parenthood

The great dilemma in being a parent is the contradiction between wanting to raise our children to be independent and wanting to keep them dependent on us long enough so that they stay connected to us. One of the most perplexing questions about our own conduct is how to decide when to let go, how much freedom to allow, and how to allow it. Children's main task in life is to grow, to develop, and to learn how to live autonomously, but we humans, unlike animals, want to maintain family relationships throughout life.

We are also aware that each of our children, as they become adult, wants to become related to and connected with others, outside our own family circle. This is an added threat to us. Even when they are small, we may think of their future in-laws; wonder how our child will choose a spouse, and what effect that will have upon us. We wonder if we will still be important to them and worry that they may prefer parents-in-law to us. Some of us cherish dreams that our children will unite with the daughters and/or sons of our good friends, thereby connecting all of us in one family circle.

We crave continuing relationships, but with no guarantee that our children will want our companionship as they grow up, we are reluctant to help them separate from us. In the beginning, as we undertake the responsibilities of parenthood, we hope for the future. We still have some of the expectations our ancestors had that if we take care of our children when they are small, they will take care of us when we are old. Our common sense shows us, however, that this is no longer universally true. We wonder how to assure the continuity between ourselves and the next generation. In our anxiety for such continuity, we sometimes cling to our children in ways that may destroy the very relationship we want to preserve.

Betty Johnston, mother of four daughters, spoke to me about her children's independence from her:

"I've invested a lot of myself into my children, and I don't see that it's necessary for a kid to be so independent all the time. I feel that by investing time now, I'm building for the future. Our goal is for each of our children to grow into an independent adult, but we also want to maintain a family feeling. Doing things together is part of that. I don't want to cut them off."

She was talking about the necessity for letting go, and the different ways a parent shares in a child's time and activities. For instance, the parent is often a teacher, but some things a child learns to do forever, while other skills may offer the kinds of activity in which a parent can continue to participate.

When you teach a child to brush her teeth, she knows how forever after. You may want to remind her, but you don't have to give additional instruction. After an infant learns to drink from a cup, he can always do it. As a toddler he may want the nipple he sees in the mouth of another infant, but he is able to drink from a glass or cup. Once they learn to tie their shoelaces, they can tie any kind of cord thereafter. The basic movements of laying one cord over another are there and available when they want to tie Boy Scout knots or to do macrame.

Mrs. Johnston recalled examples of different kinds of learning. When her youngest child was an infant, the older ones enjoyed teaching her to move around. She might have learned to crawl without help, but they helped her a lot when she was learning to walk. Once she learned to walk alone, she did not again need to be carried around. Occasionally she wanted to be carried in someone's arms, but everybody knew she could walk alone. However, after she learned to cross the streets alone near her home, she still could not cross alone at the busiest intersection in town. There she needed the company of a parent or older sister until she gained enough experience so she could manage alone.

Crossing the street alone in our high-traffic society is symbolic for many parents—and probably for their children. It is one of the first visible signs of independence and may set the tone for later trials. Within this act are many of the components of "letting go:" the danger, the trust, the separation, and the ultimate confidence the child gains, knowing that she or he can venture alone into the world outside the home.

For many adults, one of their earliest recollections is of a saunter into the street. The consequences vary but the circumstances may recur in similar ways throughout life. One man recalls running out of the house in his underwear when he was very small into a street piled high with snow barricades. A woman remembers dropping her mother's hand to get closer to the street where fresh tar was being laid so that she could savor the smell.

Another symbolic act in our culture is shopping alone. As children approach the teen years and the time of rapid growth, supplying their clothing often becomes a source of family conflict. On the one hand, the parents with budget limitations and practical considerations, and on the other, a child who constantly outgrows his or her sleeves and pant-legs and wants new clothes just like everybody else's.

At this point parents typically allow young people to make minor purchases without consultation but still go along when it is time to make a major purchase like a winter coat. Mrs. Johnston, in discussing her own role in her daughters' independence, pointed out that sometimes she likes to go with them on a shopping trip just for the sense of companionship and sharing in an event, but it is a comfort to her to know that she doesn't have to go with them all the time.

She expresses her own feeling of a loss of power when she realizes she is not needed as much as she used to be. She says: "When she's on her own, and you see that she has the ability, there's a sense of pride that she has the independence, but there's also a feeling of loss of power, of helplessness and not being able to control any more. Then you're in a different position. The very idea that your child can be your equal in some ways is very hard to take."

Her feelings certainly are shared by many parents, especially mothers who derive great satisfaction from the feeling that their children need them very much. A large insurance company has made such situations a model for their television commercials, showing fathers how much they are needed as an incentive to purchase life insurance.

As children become independent, fathers and mothers are faced with the loss of such satisfaction. This happens regardless of whether the parent has actually fostered independence. There is still an effect when the child first walks alone and can walk away from other people as easily as to walk toward them. We fear he will walk away from us too soon.

Each succeeding event in the child's development affects the parent. The mixture of pride and loss accompanies the first day of school, the first day at camp, the first trip away from home without parents, as well as the movement of an adult daughter or son away from home to college, to work, or to a different dwelling.

In each instance we are aware that our offspring can choose whether to walk away from us completely or to walk toward us from time to time.

As I said earlier, however, animal parents turn their offspring loose at a very early age, although there is some evidence that certain species maintain something like family connections in the herd. We can't compare animal feelings of loss and/or separation with our own for we don't know whether animals have feelings. We only know for certain that we do, and that our feelings are individual within each one of us, even though many of them are universal. It is the specific combinations of feelings at specific moments that are unique to each of us. We run the whole gamut from wanting to keep our children with us and dependent on us for their entire lives, to the other extreme of wanting them to be independent at the earliest possible moment. The dangers of both positions are often hidden from us. Dr. Alvin F. Poussaint in the Chicago *Sunday Sun-Times* of October 1, 1978, writing about so-called "good" parents, says:

At the opposite extreme from neglectful parents, are the overly concerned and overly conscientious ones who are so afraid of making a mistake that they stifle their children's growth. . . . Some parents also want their children to be perfect, and therefore they make subtle demands for exceptionally proper behavior.

It is the rare parents who can teach their children to be independent, let them go forward perhaps to stumble, and then take the chance that those independent children will still choose a reciprocal affinity for their parents, still want to maintain family ties.

We know that some parents feel that children are too much bother and look upon them as burdens to be cast off fast. The evidence of this is in those youngsters who are abandoned to become the responsibility of the public. Others growing up in a home with one or both parents receive the barest minimum of care for survival. Their children may realize just how little they are accepted. Whether they try hard to gain approval from their parents or rebel against them, becomes the individual choice of the children. Sometimes two children in the same family make different choices, one devoting his whole life to seeking approval from one or both parents, the other choosing to make her own life completely separate, often at a great distance.

Lila Yanow, mother of an adult daughter who has left home to live on the other side of the world, said to me: "I wanted her to be independent, but she's becoming independent within herself. I wish she could be independent but still be with us in the family unit."

That daughter has a mother whose whole life is bound up in her children; she feared the day they would leave the nest. Such a parent often clings to a child long after the child is an adult and may impose "mother-guilt" or "father-guilt." Sometimes the feeling is mutual; just as the parent doesn't want to let go, the child leans on the parent long after the time for independence.

A few years ago I observed such an alliance in a men's clothing store. A married couple who appeared to be in their late thirties came into the store with their son about thirteen and daughter about ten. With them was an older man who looked to be approaching sixty. They wanted to buy a suit for the young man to wear to a forthcoming family event. He tried on several, coming out of the fitting room each time for the others to inspect. It soon became obvious that the one person who would make the decision was the grandfather. He came forward to inspect each garment, stroking the lapels and examining the workmanship, suggesting another turn around the mirror. The younger man deferred to him completely, calling him "Papa" and actively seeking his advice. It was clear that the dependency of the younger man on his father had lasted long after he should have been independent. Although he had a wife and two nearly grown children, he still looked to his father to make a decision for him in a relatively simple activity. His own children, watching, were learning one way to become an adult—a dependent way.

I recall a similar occasion when my husband and I made a major decision without consulting anyone. With our two very young children we were at an automobile salesroom a long distance from home considering trading in our car for a new one. We wanted a speedy decision and realized that we could make it without asking anybody else, not any of our brothers who had more experience with cars than we did, nor our parents, who had lived longer and thus had more experience with family budgets, nor any of our friends who had recently purchased similar autos. It was exhilarating to realize that we could decide, and our children shared in our experience of independence.

All of us are between the extremes of holding on too long and letting go too soon. We have deep feelings about our parents and our children. We relish the dependence of our sons and daughters on us, and the resulting feeling of power, at the same time that we resent their demands and our own loss of freedom. We think that their dependence gives us control over them and that we are entitled to the glow of reflected glory from their achievements.

Similarly we seek independence from our own parents while we court their approval. Increasingly as our parents live longer we resent even the the possibility of their dependence on us. Altogether the web of family relationships may threaten to strangle, or at least to inhibit us. We are confused and long to be clear.

Mixed up with the positive feelings of affection, pride, and joy are the negative ones such as anger, fear, and resentment. We rarely stop to consider the differences in our feelings from time to time, much less to make ourselves consciously aware of the process by which they arrive within. We are more likely to want to exhibit and acknowledge the good feelings and restrain and cover up the bad ones.

To become aware of and examine our own feelings is a productive exercise. We may assume that they just "come over us" and that we are helpless in how they affect us. We ignore our own part in producing our emotions. As we learn, we become better able to control how we will be affected.

It's the rare parent coming out of some incident with a child who hasn't felt, "Why did you do this to *me*?" or "What did I do wrong? How have I failed as a parent?" or other expressions of self-defeating ideas. Or we get angry, maybe even go into a rage when a situation doesn't turn out the way we want it to. We all suffer from chronic human imperfection, and that's an incurable condition. However, knowledge can help you conquer some of the symptoms.

Let us consider the components of some of the commonest emotions:

First, those we call "negative": anger, anxiety, fear, guilt, resentment. These definitions may not be psychiatrically exactly accurate. I have chosen descriptions (paraphrased and adapted from *Webster's New Collegiate Dictionary*, Seventh Edition, and the *Psychology Encyclopedia*, Dushkin Publishing Group, Inc.) that are easily understood.

Anger: A strong feeling of displeasure and usually of hostility. Related to ire, rage, fury, indignation, wrath. At its mildest may be called "annoyance:" at its strongest, "rage." It can be aroused by the act of another person, or by the inability of one's self to act. A machine or other inanimate object that does not perform as we intend can trigger the feeling. It is one of the most often felt emotions. Some people express it in words or actions; others attempt to withhold anger, or deny feeling it. It is basic to much of our feelings and is considered to be one of the "primary affects."

Think about the last time you felt angry and what you did about it. Did it involve your child? Did you lash out? Or did you simmer inside because you were brought up to believe that it isn't "nice" or "right" to show anger? Maybe your inability to express your anger moved you to tears or to sullen coldness. Was it your own anger more than the child's misbehavior that propelled you to spank? Or were you covering up anger at your spouse that time you wouldn't talk for three days?

Anger isn't bad; it's natural. But it can be destructive. Or you can finish with it before it destroys.

Anxiety: A painful or apprehensive uneasiness of mind usually over an impending or anticipated ill; a sense of fear. This condition is what we are likely to call "worry." We worry and become anxious with good cause, but we may also worry when we feel frightened about something that may or may not happen. Feeling this way can cause us to be unable to function in the usual manner or can become a preoccupation in our minds that we carry with us all the time, or both.

Have you felt worried and/or anxious recently? Was it helpful? Did feeling anxious contribute to the solution of the problem or did it just make you feel bad? A parent worries, often unnecessarily, when a child or teen is late in arriving home. We wonder whether something terrible has happened, but in the vast majority of situations later learn that our worry was unwarranted.

Anxiety may last longer. We may feel concerned for weeks about one of our children, worrying that he or she will fail a course, or not be accepted into the "right" group, or the "right" school. Our anxiety may turn inward. Did I do enough for my son? Or did I do too much for my daughter? Anxiety is certainly inevitable when someone is critically ill and we are afraid of the outcome, but we can, with effort, eliminate from our minds much anxiety that is unnecessary.

Fear: An intense feeling of anticipation or awareness of danger or of something menacing, such as pain or injury. Fear is related to alarm, panic, fright, and trepidation and in a severe form may be experienced as dread. Fear can be a powerful emotion in the sense that the feeling of fear gives one the power to do something about it.

If you are standing in the open and see something huge, such as a moving truck, coming toward you, you will feel fear and this can push you to move out of the path of danger. Or intense fear can also paralyze you so that you cannot move. The point is that fear is a normal, sometimes logical emotion that has an effect on your body. You may experience nervous sweating, rapid breathing, tenseness or trembling of muscles, dryness of the mouth, and become aware of an increased pounding of your heart.

In our relationships with our children, we sometimes fear for their safety and are moved to action. If a small child is in a big lake or the ocean, and you the parent see a high wave coming, fear for the child's safety will move you to grasp the child and bring her or him to shore. In raising an independent child, fear for the child's safety and well-being makes it difficult to let go, to grant the necessary freedom in safe surroundings so that the child can function autonomously.

Guilt: Possibly the most universal feeling that parents experience. There is actual guilt, and there are guilt feelings. I will not discuss actual guilt, the penalty for conduct against the law or the code of human relations. That is for courts and juries to assess. What most parents experience are guilty feelings about mistakes they may have made or are likely to make in their daily lives. We all operate under standards of behavior we carry with us all the time, and we're all aware of the impressions we create on other people. In fact, we may guide ourselves too much by what we suppose other people are thinking.

We produce guilt feelings out of our excessive concern to be perfect, to "do the right thing," to earn the approval of others. Generally, the closer our relationship to other people, the more intense is our feeling of guilt when we judge we have not lived up to our own standards of behavior. Thus, feelings of guilt are strongest in relation to our spouses, partners, parents, and/or offspring. Such guilt feelings make us feel depressed, ashamed, at fault, and to blame.

To feel guilty in the absence of an illegal or immoral act is to say, "I'm really a very good person. Even if I didn't do right, at least I have the decency to feel bad about it." Or, "Look how good I am because of how bad I feel." The trouble with such statements is that while we feel guilty we are unable to function in a productive way; we are bogged down by the bad feelings and unable to summon good ones. Feeling guilty is a waste of time and effort and can be eliminated.

Resentment: Related to anger, a feeling of being indignant at something perceived as an offense. We are likely to feel resentful if we think we have received an insult, an injury to our sense of well-being. In our relationships with our kin, especially our children, we are likely to feel resentment when we think we are not sufficiently rewarded for our efforts. "Life isn't fair" may mean that "I give so much of myself, and do so much for you, and I don't get anything (or enough) in return."

A feeling of resentment is directed at someone else, or at many people, or even at the world in general, but like other negative feelings the person it harms the most is the person who feels it, for resentment doesn't help one accomplish anything of value. It merely contributes to a loss of one's self-esteem, which makes it more difficult to be a confident person capable of helpful relations with others.

All of these "negative" feelings occur in all of us from time to time, and none of them is abnormal. It is an excess of any, or any combination of them, that affects us and confounds our attempts to function as caring, giving, co-operating persons. Especially in connection with our relations with those close to us, it is effective to stop still, to examine what feelings are operating and try to see how they affect us. It is inevitable that we will experience some or all of them, but it is not inevitable that we must allow them to push us in ways we would rather not go.

But the "down" feelings are not all there is to emotions. There are also the "ups": affection, joy, pride, and the elusive feeling of contentment we call happiness. We spend our lives searching and yearning for happiness without any clear idea of what it can be and how to get it.

Affection: Also called love, related to ardor, in general a feeling of fond attachment for another person, whether or not it is reciprocated. In this kind of feeling we realize there may or may not be good reason. Sometimes we think we love in spite of, rather than because of, the receiving person's qualities. The range is great, as it is with all emotions, from a mild feeling of kinship to the intense feelings usually reserved for those closest to us.

Before our children are born we wonder whether we will be able to love such an unknown entity. When they are infants their total dependence on us may trigger the most overpowering feelings of attachment to them. When they get old enough to misbehave, however, it sometimes becomes doubtful whether we can love them continuously through all their mischief. "I love you, but I don't like what you do" may be a difficult statement to make, but it is crucial to a child's sense of self.

It is our affection for our children that sometimes operates to hinder their independence. Our love for them, and our desire to receive their love makes us want to keep them near us. Like Mrs. Johnston quoted above, we want an ongoing connection with them throughout our lives.

Joy: Everything good seems bound up in this one. It's a feeling of gaiety, the experience of delight. It's generally produced by some success or good fortune. It accompanies the birth of a child and the experience of many of life's milestone events. There's no point to defining it; everybody knows what it is and wants more of it. The limitations are important, since life does not offer joy to us constantly, and we must recognize that it is precious when it comes. Particularly it is essential that as parents we realize that we cannot expect our children to provide it for us.

We do often feel joy as a result of our children's growth and development, but to expect it is folly. For we do not own our children. We have the responsibility for their care, nurture, and support until they can function alone, but even though they do bring us joy from time to time that is not their main purpose in life. Our children will be free to become independent if we realize the limitations of their debts to us.

Pride: Often coupled with the foregoing "joy" in terms of parents' connection to children and similarly limited. Pride also arises from possession, as though the child's attainments or achievements belong to the parent. It is inevitable to feel proud of one's child on occasion, but it is damaging to demand that one's offspring be a source of pride. To make such demands is to set up a situation in which the child will either rebel against the expectations or try very hard to meet them and feel like a failure if he or she does not.

Furthermore, life is an ongoing process, and the excessive pride you feel today may lead to tomorrow's downfall.

The precious quality of life we all yearn for is that we describe as "happiness." It's an ongoing state of pleasure, well-being and satisfaction. When we were all little children, we thought we'd find happiness when, like the characters in stories, we found a mate with whom to live happily ever after. Becoming adults, we realize life is not so simple, but we still crave to be happy. Our mistake is in expecting such happiness to come toward us as if it were a moving vehicle seeking a target or as if it were a tangible pile of something just waiting to be found, when in fact happiness is a state attainable only when we can accept imperfection in ourselves, in others, and in life. When we change our expectations and our perceptions, we also change the quality of our lives.

This does not attempt to be a complete and thorough analysis of all the feelings a person can have. It is merely to point out that a variety of emotions operate in each of us and either contribute to or detract from our abilities to live as we think we want to. All emotions are produced by the person who feels them, even though it doesn't seem that way, and even though we may think we suffer from feelings we don't actually want.

Why bother to try to understand your own feelings? Because very often we know what we ought to do or say, but find it very difficult to perform and follow through.

Something within seems to stop us, and all we have left are good intentions. That "something within" is the emotional component of our behavior. Simply knowing what to do isn't enough—we have to learn how to do it, and the first step is to uncover our own feelings about ourselves and our relations with others, especially our children.

With that understanding, what can a parent do? Realize that emotions are the fuel for the human engine. Feelings of intensity propel us towards greater action or halt us into immobility. It is possible to turn off the engine, even for a moment, and think about what is happening, to realize that there is a purpose for which we have produced the fuel. We may not always be able to decide just how to feel, but we can decide how to act and what to say. With practice, such decisions become easier to make and more productive of the outcome we really want.

The paradox of parenthood is the problem of making decisions, and when we understand the feelings that underlie all our behavior, we are more able to function without the contradictions that are paradox.

chapter six

Illness and Handicaps

Raising a child means coping with illness, real and questionable, mild to severe. Every parent endures the worry, indecision, and extra work that comes from a child's sickness. From the first days of new parenthood, when a conscientious father or mother may hang over the bassinet to make sure the baby is breathing, to the years of the children's teens when one worries whether football inevitably means broken bones, parents feel the heavy responsibility of taking care of their children. This usually means having many different feelings about the child: fear for the consequences of the illness, concern over handling it properly for the welfare of the youngster, and annoyance at the inconvenience it causes.

We know that children are prone to all sorts of aches, pains, and fevers, but if we have any doubts, there are statistics to inform us. As a result of a National Health Survey conducted around 1960, the U.S Department of Health, Education and Welfare* tells us a few things about

*U. S. Department of Health, Education and Welfare; Welfare Administration, Children's Bureau, 1963. "Illness Among Children." Data from U. S. National Health Survey by Clara G. Schiffer and Eleanor P. Hunt, Child Health Studies Branch.

illness in childhood. Although this survey was done almost two decades ago, there is little evidence to show
that its data is no longer valid. In addition to the information about the prevalence of illness, the survey sorted
out illness and handicapping conditions according to the
range of restriction each imposes on a child's activities.

It was found that there was an average of eleven days
each year per child under fifteen years old in which,
because of acute illness and/or injury, children were unable to engage in their usual activities. This includes hospitalization days, and it is calculated that almost five of
the eleven days of restricted activity were spent in bed.
It was further found that there was an average of three
episodes of acute illness per year for every child with
respiratory conditions accounting for the largest single
group of conditions reported.

Respiratory conditions, of course, include all the common colds and influenza, as well as asthma and allergic
manifestations. Casual observation tells us the same
thing. We also know that no individual child will fit into
the average. Three colds a year means that some children
will have five or six, and others perhaps only one. A
statistical average gives us only general trends and is not
to be applied as a measurement to any one person.

In addition to sickness, there was an average of slightly
less than one medically attended injury per year for every
three children, resulting in restriction of activity. In ordinary language, that means that nearly one out of every
three children each year will be injured in such a way as
to be slowed down for a while. These figures are ac-
knowledged to be imprecise, but they are at least an in-
dication of what a parent can expect.

Besides acute illness and injury, there is also the problem of chronic illness in children. New drugs and preventive immunization have removed from childhood the epidemics of earlier times when parents had to watch their children suffer from and sometimes die of ailments such as poliomyelitis, rheumatic fever, diphtheria, and measles. Even if children did recover, they might be crippled for the rest of their lives. Nevertheless, many other childhood chronic illnesses continue to attack children, and every parent must somehow deal with their effects.

Some of the commonest of the chronic conditions are orthopedic impairments, sight and hearing deficiencies, speech defects, heart and lung diseases. There are congenital conditions, those that exist at birth, even though they may not immediately be recognized, and the later conditions which occur as a result of disease or injury. We need not name them all, but only recognize that anything less than optimum health affects the condition, behavior, and outlook of the child and requires additional care, knowledge, and concern from a parent.

Our interest here is in how a parent treats the child in order to enhance rather than diminish the child's sense of independence, for illness is only one of the stresses of life that affect the way a child grows and develops. Overcoming illness is an experience in overcoming other stumbling blocks that life sets up for all of us. Thus, the way parents conduct their relationships with their children during illness is as important as the way family life is lived daily. Although illness places additional stress on everyone, its effect on the child is not apart from "real" life, but an integral part of it. The child who falls ill is the same child who was into mischief the day before, and the same child who brought so much joy into the family just before that. The personality of the sick child remains the same.

Parents are likely to assume that when a child is ill, restricted, or handicapped, all the principles about independence have to go out the window. This is the time when a parent feels the strongest pull on the heartstrings and the greatest burden on the shoulders. A concerned father and mother truly wish that the hurt, the pain, the disability, could be theirs to bear rather than the child's. It's so hard to look at your little one—or even an adolescent, or a young adult—suffering, and still believe that the child can cope. Then, too, we're all aware that children can and often do use their discomfort to manipulate us. We can't always tell when the complaints are legitimate and when they're created for secondary gain.

"Secondary gain" is a phrase I learned from our family pediatrician. In the *Psychiatric Glossary* of the American Psychiatric Association, 1969 edition, it is described as:

> The external gain that is derived from any illness such as personal attention and service, monetary gains, disability benefits, and release from unpleasant responsibility.

Such gain is not limited to children, but in the context of this book it applies only in relation to children and young people. In any event, the gain children can get is likely to be somewhat different from the gain sought by adults. For children, the extra gain is usually the personal attention and services, plus release from unpleasant responsibility.

For example, Rhea, age nine, was accidentally knocked down by the school van that brought her home from after school activities. Her knees were badly bruised, but aside from that and being dirty and scared, she was all right. No bones were broken, no severe damage was done. But she did hurt all over. She was taken to the hospital emergency room for X-rays and then carefully examined by her own doctor who suggested a few days of complete rest. During that time, her schoolmates and friends came to visit, brought her school work, and entertained her with their company.

The next Monday she was clearly well enough to return to school, but she began to complain and to act like a martyr. Since she was normally a pleasant child eager to be active, her behavior presented a puzzle to her parents. Her doctor discussed it with her and reported to her mother that she was merely responding to the loss of attention. For nearly a week she had been holding court like a princess, and of course she enjoyed it. When she had to return to being just one of the common people, she was reluctant to give up her special position. Realizing this, her parents ceased to lavish extra attention on Rhea, and she promptly recovered. Although she was trying to get secondary gain, she was unsuccessful. Her independence was enhanced by the atmosphere that communicated to her the message that she could handle the slight disruption in her life caused by the accident. Each person needs that knowledge, and a child especially needs to know, "I can cope. I can do it."

Even as adults, all of us know that uncomfortable feeling that says, "I don't think I'm up to it." Children have more legitimate cause to feel that way, and we must be careful not to contribute to it. When we feel sorry for children, or pity them, what we do is put them down. They feel minimized by our worries about them and lose some of their own self-confidence. However, when we assume by our attitudes our own conviction that a child can manage, we give that child increased belief in himself or herself.

We must be cautious, however, not to expect a young child to take the responsibility for taking prescribed medicine when there is a diagnosed illness and a regimen for treatment. Even though a child may be able to pour the medicine into a spoon and get the spoon to her mouth to drink it, it may not be safe to rely on her to do so. When a child can tell time, it is wise to discuss the physician's instructions with him or her and suggest that the youngster watch the clock for the time to take medicine. But a responsible adult has to be prepared to be ready to step in on time if the child forgets. After the age of about twelve, the youngster who has been growing up to be independent can probably take the responsibility for his or her own care. If, however, there is an ongoing conflict between the young person and the parent, the illness will be affected by it. In such a situation, one must look to the solution of the conflict.

Illness may be a ploy to gain release from responsibility—one of the "secondary gains" mentioned in the definition cited above. Although we expect our children to carry various responsibilities for their bodies and their possessions, their greatest responsibility in our culture is attending school. It follows that illness may be feigned or actually produced as a device to evade the classroom. When a child doesn't feel well, home responsibilities can also be avoided. Somebody else has to do the dishes, walk the dog, take out the garbage, or perform whatever tasks the family depends on that child to do. But staying home from school is the clearest evidence a child can have of release from responsibility. Particularly if school has been troublesome for the child, or if something unpleasant has happened there, being sick enough to stay home can become very attractive.

Some pediatricians say that their offices are filled in early fall with school-aged children who complain of stomach aches, headaches, stuffy noses, and coughs. The doctors acknowledge that the aches and pains are real, in contrast to those sometimes complained of by adults, and they have various explanations for how these come about.

Dr. Prudence Krieger, consultant on pediatric infectious diseases at Lutheran General Hospital, Park Ridge, Illinois, in an article in the *Chicago Suburban Sun-Times*, October 20, 1978, says: "Making sure kids' ears are covered and scarves are wrapped around their necks doesn't prevent them from getting sick."

Dr. Patricia Conard, pediatrician of the same town, says in the same article that young children and adolescents rarely make up illnesses. She says: "It's very important for parents to understand that stomach aches and headaches may be caused by tension." Dr. Conard says it's easier to see this tension in young children than it is as they grow older. Older children have already developed patterns for dealing with discomfort that may allow them to deceive the adults around them. With young children, the incident or situation that preceded the tension is more easily observed. A kindergartener, for instance, may be apprehensive about being away from home for the first time without a parent. A first grader may feel terrible because friends in the classroom can read already, and she can't.

Still, diagnosis is different for a parent than it is for a pediatrician. In the middle of the night, awakened by an unexpected noise coming from the child's vicinity, a parent is confronted with symptoms that can be frightening. The child may already have vomited by the time mother or father gets to the bedside. There is a massive cleanup job to do while one worries whether this is appendicitis or merely something ingested that didn't digest. The child who coughs all night, losing sleep for himself and keeping the rest of the family awake, makes a parent wonder how severe an illness causes that much distress.

First thing in the morning, when everyone in the family is getting up to meet the day, one child may complain of a very sore throat. A special problem is created if there will be no one home to stay with the sick child. Father has to go to work, Mother may also have to go to work or school, and the usual routine is that the child goes to day care or to school. If he is really ill, different arrangements need to be made for his care. However, if he is exaggerating the discomfort, it may be necessary to insist that he get up and get ready. A decision must be made that takes into account the youngster's age and capacity for independence. Can he go to day care anyway, and risk infecting other children, besides risking exposure to additional infection himself? Does he need to stay home from school, and if so, who is going to stay with him? Or is he old enough and capable enough to stay alone? No matter which decision is made, the alternatives loom threatening. One must resist the temptation to baby growing children and learn to trust their capacity to cope.

During illness, a child may revert to the behavior of a younger age, wanting more assistance and more attention. Although it's natural for this to happen, a parent must beware of the temptation to overdo service. The helpful rule to keep in mind is that you don't ever do anything for a child that he or she can do for himself or herself. This covers a lot of the activity that conscientious mothers are inclined to conduct. Even in sickness, there are still many independent activities for any child who is not completely paralyzed. For instance, instead of running to the bedside with a drink of water every time the patient feels thirsty, a bottle or pitcher of water can be provided, with a cup to fill, for a child who has already demonstrated the ability to pour. Even if the youngster wants something that is not within reach, it is usually better if he or she gets out of bed to get it than for someone to come running to do the fetching.

If there is a question in your mind about your ability to keep a sick child in bed or immobilized, you're in good company. Every parent knows how difficult it is to insist that a child stay in bed, especially if you don't intend to dance attention and service on her or him continuously. In the absence of specific instruction to the contrary, heed the words of a pediatrician, Dr. Jack G. Shiller, who writes in *Childhood Illness: A Common Sense Approach:*

> Most small children regulate their own activity very well. You cannot keep them up when they are sleepy, and they will cover seven to eight miles a day within the confines of their beds when they feel up to it. I have very few rules about keeping the sick child in or out of bed, in or out of doors.

This isn't just Dr. Shiller's own idea, however. He says further:

> Clinical studies have been made of traditional bed-rest diseases like nephritis, rheumatic fever and hepatitis; bed rest per se has been pretty well discredited. I don't mean to suggest that rest is not important. But rest can often be made much more acceptable to a child who is allowed to be up and about.

What often happens is that in the attempt to keep a child contented to stay in bed, the parent or other adult goes to great lengths of effort. An average conscientious mother will literally spend hours at the bedside reading to and otherwise entertaining a sick child. She might prepare an especially attractive tray of food complete with decorations in the hope she can persuade the child to eat. There is no end to what such a parent might do in the attempt to help the youngster be content.

But the result is often a contest in which the patient tries to see how much attention and service he or she can get, and the parent loses patience. As in many other incidents of family life, during illness one must find the common ground on which the adult performs the tasks actually necessary for the well-being of the child, and the child assumes responsibility for her or his own behavior, activity and entertainment.

If it becomes necessary for a child to enter a hospital either for treatment of an illness or for diagnostic procedures, the institution and its staff enter into the family relationships. Parents have to contend with hospital physicians and personnel whom they suspect do not share their deep concern about their own child. Of course the professionals cannot have the strong emotional connection to the children they tend that the parents do. They must maintain a certain amount of professional detachment in order to do their work. For that reason, many pediatricians will not attempt to have their own children as patients. They prefer to rely on their colleagues.

But it is well to remember that the physician, the nurse, the technician, and the other staff choose to work with children. The staff of a children's section in a hospital or of a children's hospital, is generally there precisely because they want to work with children and they care about them.

Ann M. Brush, Pediatric Nurse-Clinician at Evanston Hospital Department of Pediatrics, Evanston, Illinois, speaks of the differences she observes in children admitted to the hospital and differences in behavior of their parents:

Many mothers are very over-protective of children in the hospital. They may feel guilty, wondering "What did I do wrong?" If a child is brought into the hospital for treatment for a stomach upset, that mother may blame herself for not washing dishes thoroughly enough, or for not cooking the pork through, and take the sickness as her fault, when actually she had very little to do with it.

Ms. Brush notes that in the hospital where she is employed parents have the option of twenty-four hour "rooming-in" if they wish to stay with their children. Some parents interpret this choice as an obligation. They stay with the ill child continually and take care of her or him as they would at home. There are also parents who see the hospitalization as a misfortune that has befallen the youngster and use that for an excuse to allow gross indulgence. They bring candy and sweets in such quantity that the child refuses regular meals; that child may retard his or her own healing and/or the normal functions of the body are disturbed. Some allow the child to ignore a normal bedtime, with the resulting fatigue and crabbiness. Others lavish attention on the child far beyond what is necessary or advisable. Occasionally they even interfere with the procedures that must be performed by nurses, doctors, and technicians because they don't want the child disturbed or discomfited.

Additionally, Mrs. Brush says, adults who have themselves had bad experiences in hospitals are afraid their children will also suffer. They are watchful and sometimes antagonistic because of their fear. She says that once in a while a mother who won't leave won't trust anybody else to care for her child:

She'll stay in the hospital full time with the little one, and then lose her patience because she's exhausted.

On the other hand, children who have catastrophic illnesses may come in and out of the hospital on a fairly regular basis. The family learns to handle this kind of situation very early, and they often learn to allow such a child to be more independent in the hospital than one who is admitted as an emergency—for instance, with a ruptured appendix.

Ms. Brush says:

I have seen little girls as young as five, with a terminal disease, left alone at night with the understanding that the routine in the hospital will be pretty much what it is at home. That is, regular bedtime, no snacks after a certain hour, limits on television. That child might not survive for the next six months, but the mother will set limits as she would for a healthy child, ask us to abide by them, and we do so, as much as possible.

Such a child, she says, has a far better outlook on the hospitalization than the one who is over-indulged and over-protected. When asked what she would want from the parents of patients, she stresses the importance of cooperation between the hospital staff and parents, and the necessity for communication between them.

I would hope that the mother or father of a patient would help me explain the necessary procedure to the child. Six-year-olds have a lot more intelligence than people give them credit for. I want to know the specific words a small child uses for the parts of the body and its functions, so I can understand his or her needs if the parent isn't there.

She asks also for honesty rather than white lies. She doesn't want to be requested to tell the child that a parent is in the next room if, in fact, that parent has gone out to eat, or gone home to rest. She emphasizes that in the hospital the child is an individual, and the best possible opportunity for the staff to help the child occurs when the child can trust them. This requires honesty and forthrightness among the adults. The older the child, the more important it becomes that he or she feel competent to cope with the entire situation.

As Ms. Brush suggests, there is a distinct difference between the hospitalization of a child who becomes acutely ill or is injured in an accident, and the one who has a severe and prolonged illness and/or disability. The parents of the latter child have long-range concerns, and the child is likely to be in and out of hospitals many times. Even if the parents feel they want to protect their youngster, such an attitude isn't appropriate, and it doesn't help.

Franklin and Sylvia Lewis told me in detail about their early experiences with their son Bart, who at age fourteen is a bright active boy who excels in school and has many friends and activities despite a congenital anomaly of the circulatory system. When I asked them to tell me about their experiences and their views now as a result of them, their first response was to say they had always hoped that they could help other parents faced with similar situations. It is still difficult for them to take Bart's life for granted, but they feel satisfied with the way they have treated him and the way their relationships have developed. The comments that follow came from both the Lewises as they told me the story of Bart's health:

> The baby was just twenty-four hours old when the hospital physicians told us they suspected he was cyanotic, that is, not getting enough oxygen. He was transferred in the middle of the night to a specialized hospital where he underwent further study, and surgery was performed the next day, as soon as the problem was sufficiently understood.

I asked whether they had treated their baby with extra care, and they told me that when he was two weeks old, having been released from the hospital, they left him with a competent sitter to go out of town to the wedding of a close family member. I was surprised at this, but Sylvia told me:

> From the beginning, we were very aware that we were not going to treat Bart differently. He was our first child, so we had no prior experience to compare. The one thing we did under doctor's advice was to feed him every two hours day and night. We were told he needed every drop of nourishment because he had lost so much weight. Now I wonder whether his poor sleeping habits—he's up at least once every night—can be traced to that time.

They went on to tell me that they were determined not to treat Bart differently from other babies. They would take him everywhere or leave him with a sitter if that was more appropriate to the situation. There was one obstacle to treating him normally, however, and that was grandparents and other adults.

> We got so much disapproval. It seemed that everybody besides us was saying we should coddle him

more, protect him. But we understood the nature of his illness, and accepted it. He has an ongoing chronic deficiency. He had surgery again when he was around three, and surgery may be necessary again some time in the future. We just can't predict.

Franklin and Sylvia reiterated that the hardest thing they encountered in trying to raise their son to be an independent person with a strong character for self-reliance was the disapproval of grandparents, other relatives, and friends.

They thought we were too harsh. They said "poor kid" and "poor baby" and disapproved of us.

Sylvia tells about the time that Bart came home from the hospital after the second surgery. He sat in his little rocking chair and dropped pieces of paper tissue on the floor, expecting her to come and pick them up. She did not. Her refusal led to his anger and he sometimes cried, but she would not become his servant. In a short time, he understood that he could not command his mother to do his bidding, and he stopped dropping tissues.

Franklin commented:

We weren't going to be any different than any other parents. We had a child the same as other parents did. It wasn't going to make that great a difference in our lives. Not that it wasn't always on our minds. . . ."

To which Sylvia added:

We may have been too strict, but when I think of some of the alternatives, I wouldn't change anything. I think the way we raised him in the first two years had a great deal to do with his ability to survive the second surgery and its complications. The doctors at the time said he was a great fighter.

Both parents wanted to emphasize that although their son had specific limitations, he was not constantly sick. They knew from the beginning that he had a unique condition, and when he survived the first week of life they felt that every day beyond that was a bonus to be enjoyed.

Their second child was born during Bart's third year. Sylvia told me what life was like after Melissa was born. Bart had his second surgery during her infancy.

I would be wheeling Missy in the buggy, with the seat on top for Bart. But we would start out with Bart walking by my side. Only when he got tired, after a few blocks, did I pick him up to sit on the buggy seat and rest.

Of course Bart's condition is not a common one. There are many variations on serious illness that affect children, and in many cases babies and children with chronic conditions need more continuous care than Bart actually required. But the attitude that parents adopt in treating a sick youngster and the actual behavior of the people around the child have an effect not only on the child's personality but on the child's confidence in her or his own ability to survive and to cope with the consequences of the illness.

When your child is not enjoying perfect health and physical condition—which may be every day, or only a few times a year—you're not a bad parent if you're frightened, anxious, worried and/or angry. It's natural for you to have conflicting thoughts and feelings about how to treat and relate to your youngster. But no matter how you feel, you can use your good sense to do and say what will help the child most.

Besides the illnesses that respond to treatment or to hospital procedures, including surgery, there are those disabilities that do not heal, do not improve. Some children will go through life blind, or deaf, speechless, or immobilized in a wheelchair; some will have multiple afflictions. The public has finally become aware of the needs of such special children, especially for individualized educational opportunities. It is largely because of devoted parents that legislation has been passed and facilities created to offer oppportunities for healing and learning.

But as with all other children, handicapped children need as many chances as they can handle to grow into independent autonomous human beings, caring for themselves to the extent of their abilities, and encouraged to stretch to do whatever they can. Feeling sorry for them does not contribute to their growth or self-assurance. It only makes them feel more inferior. They need, as we all do, to believe in themselves as thriving human beings who belong in the world and can fit into it.

Most parents are grateful that they are not confronted with catastrophic illness in their children, but for those who must deal with it, it is good to remember that if you contribute to greater dependence in the child, you make it that much harder for him or her to enjoy life.

Part of the burden of parenting is caring for children who cannot care for themselves. In the absence of illness, this burden lightens as the child grows and learns to take care of more and more of her or his own needs. It is especially heavy when a baby, child, or adolescent is ill, but the same principle applies in health as in sickness: Don't do anything for a child that he or she can do for himself or herself. Thus a parent encourages the young one to believe in his or her own abilities, and prepares him or her to surmount the ordinary difficulties of daily

living as well as the consequences of illness, mild or
severe, temporary or permanent.

chapter seven

The Child Outside the Home and Family

Sooner or later, the child ventures outside the usual living situation at home with parents and/or family to spend a few hours, a few days, weeks, or months away from home. Although it may seem that parents, thus separated from the child, have no effect on the success of such ventures, they do in fact have a great influence before, during and afterward.

As I have been saying, the parent who clings to a child, no matter what the reason, is running the risk of thwarting the child's natural surge toward independence. This does not mean that a parent ought to cast the child out alone into the world. The task of parenthood is to let go gradually and carefully, but the dilemma of parenthood is in knowing how to let go, when to do it, and how much freedom to allow.

Experiences away from home can be valuable or discouraging. In order for them to be valuable, from the earliest days it is necessary for parents to choose carefully the kind of experience to which the child is to be exposed, to make as thorough an investigation as possible of the people and/or institutions to which the child is to be entrusted, and then to adopt an attitude that contributes to the success of the separation. Such an attitude conveys to the child the message, "You'll be okay. I know you can handle this."

If a parent expresses many doubts about the child's ability to function away from home, or if a parent hovers closely over the child waiting for the tears of farewell, the child receives a message that says, "You're so little I can't bear to see you go. You may not be able to cope with it." This message may be transmitted even to a young adult leaving at age eighteen. Some parents don't want to acknowledge that their children can function independently (without them), no matter how old they are. Each child probably has doubts anyway about venturing out into unfamiliar territory. The parent need not reinforce those doubts with additional misgivings.

In today's changing society an infant sometimes leaves the home for most of the day, to be cared for by other persons while the parent or parents are busy elsewhere. A child has a right to two parents, a mother and a father, and one need not necessarily be more important than the other, but we recognize that the family situation may not provide an ideal arrangement. It is no longer held as absolutely true that an infant must be cared for by one primary person in order to develop normally. Some infants leave the home as early as six weeks to be cared for elsewhere without damage. In the wealthy homes of the past, a nanny took over the infant at birth, and often many surrogates shared in the child care. Today, parents must decide how to fit the infant into their lives and how to provide for appropriate care. If this means some kind of day care, it may still be beneficial to everyone, if the persons who care for the infant share the parents' values and standards and give the baby or toddler personalized individual attention when it is required. Family day care, in which people take several children into their home to be cared for in the absence of parents, can offer an infant, besides the necessary care, the benefits of the company of other children of various ages, in some ways replicating the extended family.

An established order for daily life is necessary for an infant or very young child to thrive in such a situation. It is important for the developing youngster in any situation to know what to expect and who can be trusted. Therefore if the very young one is to leave the home, a regular routine for sleeping, waking, eating, and personal care, together with the devotion of the parent or parents during the time at home, helps the child learn the difference between home and the other place, and between parents and other caregivers. Some parents discover that when their hours with their infants or children are curtailed, they enjoy them more and feel freer to devote more of themselves to the family needs. In order for any child to become confident and independent, the people and the surroundings must be dependable. Parents whose very young children leave the home may need to be more aware of their responsibilities to supply order than is likely to be the case when one parent is at home all day with the infant or young child.

Not too long ago the benefits of association with other children were provided within the family circle, in a time when aunts and uncles gathered together every Sunday with their children. In general, families are smaller now and dispersed over a wider area so that this kind of gathering is rare. In the close daily association of family day care children can learn the advantages and disadvantages of rubbing against and playing with their peers.

Whatever decision you make after you have decided that neither parent will be at home continuously to take care of your infant, consider all the alternatives and choose the one that best meets your standards. Perhaps there is a grandmother or other relative available who offers to take care of the baby. Rather than jump at such an offer, consider the obligations you will incur, and consider also the environment in which the baby will spend the time. This may not be the best arrangement you can make, or on the other hand, it may be the closest thing to your own home that you can get.

If there is a day nursery available to you that cares for many infants, look into their operating procedures, the quality of the personnel employed, and the general atmosphere of the place before you decide to trust your child to them. Of course you know to see whether the facilities are clean and sanitary; I'm calling attention to the intangibles of human interaction. The alternative to staying home with the child need not be detrimental either to the baby or to the parent-child relationship. In some ways it can benefit all of you: the infant gains from the companionship of other children, even just watching them; the parents gain the freedom to pursue their own plans. The child who very early becomes accustomed to being cared for by others and surrounded by other children is likely to be making the foundation for successful entrance into the larger world of school and community. To be separated from parents can then become a natural recurring event rather than an occasion for trauma.

If you have chosen an alternate to caring for the child at home, become acquainted or better acquainted with the person or persons who will actually care for him or her, and tell them what your requirements are. Even if the caregiver is the grandmother or aunt, be sure to talk this over. If your standards cannot be met, it is better to break off arrangements early than to engage in conflict later. Get a clear understanding of how the baby is to be fed, handled, and what stimulation will be provided, for every baby needs to be part of an active lively atmosphere. To keep a child in a crib from morning until evening does not contribute to the development of optimum intellectual, emotional, and physical growth. At the very least, a baby needs to be moved from the crib to another spot, to be spoken to, and to have the opportunity to look at different things, other people, and listen to different sounds.

As the child grows and learns to move around alone, it is necessary for her or him to have more chance to explore. To keep a child always confined in a playpen or behind a fence is to inhibit growing curiosity and lose the chance to teach what is touchable and what is not. At this stage, close surveillance is necessary so that a toddler is not endangered in the investigation of electrical connections, stoves, heat, heights, sharp objects, or other hazards. If you're not going to be present to see that all these standards are met, find out what your alternate intends to do and what his or her ideas about child care include.

The quality of the relationship between parent or parents and child is of course the most important. When the time for their interaction is limited, as it must be if the parents are occupied during the day and the child is cared for by someone else, concentrated effort can make the few hours, usually in the evening, enjoyable for all. You can communicate to your child your interest in and love for her or him and make that short time special in all your lives by concentrating on family interaction and mutual participation in whatever you do. This does not mean that the child shares your every waking moment—in fact there will be times when parents crave the intimacy and privacy that can only be attained after the child retires. You are not a "bad" parent if you put a young one to bed early occasionally.

The needs of the youngsters have to fit into the schedule of the adults, and a system that everyone knows makes this feasible. Consistency is to be sought, but this does not mean that an occasional departure from routine is destructive. The ideal would be for a constant daily schedule to be in effect so that children—even infants—can sense what's going to happen next, but nobody's life is ideal. Life cannot go on as if there were no children, but neither do the adults have to devote their entire lives and efforts to the welfare of the children.

Especially for the infant or very young child who spends time away from home, the hours spent there on return can be rich and fruitful. Everyone needs to have a sense of belonging to and with other people, and it is in the family that we first learn that feeling. Without it, one can go through life feeling like an outsider, making it difficult to enjoy friendship and teamwork. With the feeling of belonging, which implies cooperation and participation, a growing young person can feel at home anywhere, with anybody, and thus comfortable and at home with herself or himself.

For the infant who stays at home to be cared for by a parent or someone in place of a parent, when he or she is around three, you may consider a play group, preschool or nursery school. Whatever arrangement you choose, your primary purpose is not just to get the child out from underfoot for a while. True, freedom from a toddler even for a few hours is a relief, but if the child assumes that is the main reason for his or her adventure, he or she may cling to home and be extremely reluctant to leave at this time and later too. No one likes to feel unwanted, especially a child, and it is very easy for a child to make that interpretation, even in error. If you think of your freedom as a welcome change for the child too, you are less likely to incur his or her reluctance to leave.

Almost as soon as a child can stay dry all night, there are likely to be invitations to "sleep over" at someone else's house. Outside of relatives, this may be the first introduction to a slightly different pattern of living, slightly different family arrangements, a strange bed, or even sleeping on the floor. Successfully accomplished, "sleeping over" can be another taste of independent living. The return engagement, when the friend is invited to your house, is also an opportunity for your youngster to act as host or hostess, to acquire status in the family as a person with friends outside the family circle. Often children in the position of host or hostess will display their competence in performing household duties, as much to impress the friend as to show their parents their capability.

The possibility of day camp in the summertime also occurs about this time. To many people summer camps are degraded as a device to keep children out of the house, but they have distinct advantages in building independence and self-confidence in children, besides giving them the opportunity to learn skills and activities not provided during the rest of the year.

In the *Parents' Yellow Pages: A Dictionary by the*

Princeton Center for Infancy (New York: Anchor/Double-day, 1978) the editors, led by Frank Caplan, comment:

> Day camp is a gradual step in building independence
> and self-confidence in children, especially beneficial
> for those who do not separate from home and parents
> easily.

It isn't necessary for children to be programmed and entertained throughout their waking hours, but neither is it conducive to their development for them to be parked in front of the television, or, by whining, "There's nothing to do" become the butt of mother's discontent. Many mothers dread the summer because they feel a responsibility to make a schedule for their children that will keep them occupied throughout the day. As in other things, there is a middle path.

If the family's finances or the community's resources do not permit a day camp experience, several families can join to form a group so that no one parent is constantly on duty. Such a group can plan outings as well as daily supervised activities and free play. Parents rotate in responsibility so that each has some time away from the children while the others are in charge of the group. Even without a group, it is worthwhile to make available specific space where children can enjoy themselves in spontaneous activity without continual supervision. The objective is to avoid situations where the parent in charge is constantly harassed by the needs and demands of a child or children, for the consequence of such harassment is likely to be yelling or screaming. Although many parents justify their conduct, I have yet to meet any who really wants to yell, scream, or hit their children.

When a child leaves home for even a few hours a day, he or she gains from the association with others, from the leadership of different adults, and in the acquisition of new skills. Not the least of the advantages of day camp, as of other separations, is the experience of leaving home and gaining the confidence that home and its dear ones will be awaiting one's return. Separation from parents is one of the most difficult tasks a young person has to do. All of us know adults who have never mastered that task. The earlier training starts in separation and return, the better it is for everybody.

Porter Sargent's *Guide to Summer Camps and Summer Schools* (Boston, Mass. 17th Ed. 1971) speaks of summer programs thus:

> The summer program movement is a momentous educational innovation, perhaps America's chief contribution to education. Summer programs effectively provide answers to the educational development of thousands of boys and girls ranging from primary to college age.

At the moment of departure, some children will inevitably cling, reluctant to leave the security of home and mother, father, or caregiver. Many, after they board the bus and it leaves the block, will stop crying. Home is out of sight and an exciting adventure beckons to them. But others will cry much more, frightened of the need to be independent. The responses vary, just as the children vary.

A larger step away is the sleep-away camp, and as the step is larger, so is the chance for growth in independence. In order for the child to make such growth, parents have to allow the release. This means that before you make any arrangements, you have to check out the camp, including not only the physical facilities and arrangements for safety, but the quality of the staff, from the director to the cabin counselors. Ideally, visit the camp and see for yourself. You may not always be able to do as thorough a job as you would like, but it is essential to know the basic accommodations and especially to inquire about the philosophy of the director and to compare it with your own.

If it is an institutional camp supported by a social agency or a religious body, you can easily find out its goals and purposes. If it is a private camp, operated for profit, it may be harder to learn what you want to know. But the directors of such camps often make their time and themselves available to parents in order to sell the season. This is a good time to ask all your questions, before you sign up. It's especially valuable to ask about the camp among people you know who have sent their children there. Your own acquaintances are more reliable sources of information than the names a camp director gives you, but do not overlook any chance to talk to other parents about the camp. After you sign the contract and pay the deposit, it's hard to change your mind.

In their *Parents' Guide to Summer Camps* (New York: Harper & Row, 1968) Charlotte M. Shapiro and Lore Jarmul answer the question "Why send your child to camp?" with the following statement:

> Outdoor life and camping refresh the child in body and mind and serve as a welcome pause after the pressures of the school year.
>
> But there is much more to camp than fresh air, sunshine, and nature. A summer away from parents, family and neighborhood friends is an important experience in the growing process. . . . At camp . . . the child must cope with the realities of his independence as a person without the security of family and friends. Still, the fun of camp activities, the com-

panionship of many children, and the presence of friendly counselors usually make for a gratifying summer.

As you consider whether to arrange for one week, two weeks, a month or the season, be honest with yourself and your youngster. Your financial situation will influence your decision, even though many non-profit camps have some scholarships available. You must consider, "Is my child ready to be away from home?" You can't always be certain. You may not think so, but the child might blossom in a different environment where expectations are different.

Keep in mind, too, that if the child senses that you don't want to let him or her go, he or she may play into your fears by saying "no" to the new experience. The accepted term for the child's reluctance is "separation anxiety." It's applied to the initial clinging to home as well as to the state of mind away from home that we call "homesickness." Every child feels it to some degree, and every parent hopes that the child is not too eager to get away.

In *The Camp Physician's Manual* by David Goldring, M.D. (Springfield, Ill.: C.C. Thomas, 1967) in a chapter on psychological disorders, Alex H. Kaplan, M. D., says:

While it is generally felt that children are upset because of the separation from the parents, often the child feels guilty because he is glad to be away from home and thoroughly enjoying himself.

A young man I know, who worked for several years as a counselor at an eight week summer camp, told me:

Kids mature more at camp. Many of them come to camp spoiled, never having done anything for themselves. At camp they have to make their own beds, help set tables, clean up around the cabin, and share in the work of the group. They develop a sense of responsibility towards themselves and others.

He also expressed the opinion that the changes in the child after one summer may not be great, but that the cumulative effect of several summers has a massive impact on the child's personality. The child learns to function autonomously in a different world and carries the abilities thus learned back home.

Another kind of travel away from home and family occurs more frequently in modern times than earlier. A child may go a long distance to see a parent if there has been a divorce, or to see grandparents who live far away, or even to visit friends who have moved away. Major airlines take notice of such travel. Each one makes its own regulations about whom they will accept unescorted and under what conditions. Their restrictions vary from one airline to the other, but in general, no airline will accept a child under the age of five without an escort, preferably an adult.

Making such a trip alone can be a valuable experience for a child. When you make the arrangements, be as specific as you can about the procedure, and tell the child every detail of how the trip is to be made. Do this because the more information a youngster has, the less room there is for doubt and fear. Verify carefully the time and place of departure and arrival, and see that the child carries ample identification as well as the exact itinerary to be followed. Without such safeguards, the child may mistakenly get the idea that she or he is being cast out into unwilling independence. The objective is to help the child feel competent to undertake the trip with the assistance of other adults as necessary.

I have been writing until now about the kind of departure from home that a young child makes, returning later to the home. The final departure is the one a young adult makes that often begins at about age eighteen with the trip to college. Increasingly, young people who do not go to college, but enter the world of work, as well as young people who attend local colleges move away from home to live apart from parents. After such separations, returns to the home are more like visits. The future promises permanent separation in an independent adult life. By this time parents have used up most of their influence and have limited control over their offspring's decisions. Probably the major control left to parents is financial. They can set limits on what they will spend and what they will pay for and refuse to support decisions of which they do not approve.

The other path, to continue to give financial support indefinitely, contributes to the continued dependence of young people who ought by that time to be moving close to complete independence. Know what you value, figure out what you can afford, and communicate these facts to the young person. It is not helpful for the parent, the son, the daughter, or the family relationships for financial dependence to continue indefinitely. If there is cooperation between the generations, and a clear understanding of the mutual goals, there is much less likely to be an abrupt and painful separation at a later date.

What if the separation experience is not successful? This can happen at any time, from infancy through the teens, but it doesn't mean the end of independence. The very value of an unsuccessful outcome at an early age lies in the fact that it is still acceptable to come home and seek comfort. One unpleasant experience—at camp, for instance—doesn't mean the whole idea was wrong. It may mean that a wrong choice was inadvertently made, that the experience was inappropriate for the child at that particular time, or that some unexpected event disrupted the season. Such an unexpected event can vary from an outbreak of illness at a sleep-away camp to an outbreak of stormy weather at a day camp. At an older age, the choice of college and environment may have been a poor one. Don't attempt to establish blame or guilt, but recognize that errors are made, natural events occur, and human beings can only go on from that point to learn from the experience and continue to grow.

Throughout childhood and its attendant separations, parents' tasks change, but their responsibilities to their children remain constant. In general, responsibility is greatest in the earliest years, as in other areas of life. The concerned parent investigates thoroughly in advance, trusts the child and the caregiver to act together in enhancing the child's growth and development, and stays out of their interaction as much as possible. "Staying out" means expressing your respect for your child and your belief in her or his competence to cope.

The parent who continually telephones, visits, and checks on the child does not contribute to the success of the experience. The child away from home does need to know that he or she is missed, but not to the point of maudlin complaints. The child away from home for more than a few days welcomes mail from home that is interesting to read and brings news, but may not even bother to read letters of advice or complaint, just as the child at home learns to turn off the repeated lectures given by parents. Don't expect much mail in return. My own experience in corresponding with our children at camp was that if they wrote a lot of letters they weren't taking advantage of involvement in camp activities. This happened usually at the beginning of the season. At that time they wrote to fight loneliness and to remind themselves about home. As the season progressed mail became scarcer. This was a good sign, for it meant that the youngster was too busy swimming, playing tennis and baseball, rehearsing for shows, or working in the craft shop. The time set aside for rest and quiet was used to catch up on other things that were more fun than writing dutiful letters home. I imagine that when camp life was at its best, days passed without a thought of home.

On the advantages of the camp experience, each of our children has said that being away from home at summer camp made it much easier to go away to college and function away from home for much longer periods of time.

Each adventure away from home, from the two hours of nursery school to the semester of college, can be an event in the gradual movement toward independence. Not all of them will be successful, but without them it is much more difficult for a child to practice his or her own competence. It is far better for the independent experience to come early, when it is acceptable to come back and crawl up on a lap for comfort. Too many children have their first experience at independent living in their very late teens when they leave home for school, and fall apart at the mere prospect of doing their own laundry for the first time.

When parents begin to let go early and gradually, they find that their children gain confidence to function independently, and then willingly stay in touch with their parents as close personal friends long after they reach maturity. Those who have been held in tight throughout their childhood and adolescence may feel it necessary to rebel by breaking away completely, scorning their parents' values and standards, and putting irrevocable distance between the generations.

If you want, as do most parents, to maintain warm contact with your children throughout your lifetime, try to give them ample opportunity to function away from you when they are young, meanwhile maintaining the security of the family circle. Then when they grow up you have much better opportunities to stay friendly.

chapter eight

Misbehavior– What to Do About It

Even the child who is learning to be independent will misbehave sometimes. As a matter of fact, what we call "misbehavior" is sometimes the experimentation a young child engages in to find out what kinds of behavior are acceptable and what kinds are not. We call it misbehavior when we feel upset: angry, hurt, frightened, and/or resentful. Our response then varies according to the intensity of our feelings at the moment, so that the child sometimes continues to test us to measure our response.

The concept of misbehavior varies from one family to another, but every parent has some standards he or she expects to uphold. In addition there are community standards, laws and ordinances regulating the conduct of everyone. The question arises as to how to act, what to do, so that our children will uphold those standards and live by them.

Often, when parents think about misbehavior, they think in terms of "naughty," "disobedient," or "bad." Putting such labels on it doesn't help to solve the problem and may make it worse. A child will quickly apply the label to herself or himself, thinking, "I'm a bad girl," or

"I'm a naughty boy," or "I'm inferior; I'm supposed to obey." Such a self-concept defeats the child and defeats the purpose of child training, which is to help him or her grow up with confidence and independence. By branding the child, you discourage her or him and give cause for them to live up to the expectations of the label. There was an old saying, "If I have the name, I might as well have the gain." Children may never have heard that phrase, but they may proceed that way nevertheless. The "bad girl" will assume that she can't be good and may give up trying. The "naughty boy" perceives that his route to significance is in being naughty and continues to travel that way. Obedience means that one person carries out the commands and instructions of another, which is only possible in a superior-inferior relationship.

Such feelings of inferiority about one's self carry over into all areas of life. The youngster will have them with him or her not only within the family, but in school and the larger community. The person who feels inferior has difficulties carrying out assignments, making friends, and in general succeeding in life.

In the dictionary, misbehavior is called improper behavior. Punishment, which often follows misbehavior, is described as the suffering, pain, or loss that serves as retribution. The two should be separated from one another because punishment has never been shown to be effective in preventing future misbehavior. It may help temporarily, but eventually, in the absence of other corrective measures, the effect wears off and misbehavior occurs again.

What actually happens within the home and family? A child does something he or she is not supposed to do, and a parent retaliates. The child may or may not know that it was wrong, depending on previous events. What the child learns when the parent retaliates is not only that it was wrong, but that the parent is bigger, more powerful, and able to inflict a sentence of judgment. This gives the child the idea that it's all right to exert your size and power on someone else, especially someone smaller. Many parents discover that when their children grow to be as big as the parents, or bigger, parents can no longer issue punishment. But even when it works, giving a youngster evidence of inferiority and/or insignificance does not contribute to the feelings necessary for healthy growth toward independence.

Even in our criminal justice system, doubt is cast on the effectiveness of punishment. One thing that can be said for it is that it serves as retribution, a penance for whatever crime was committed. Even so, the penance does not undo the crime, repair the damage, or contribute to the well being of the society at large. On the contrary, society has to pay the cost of the penance in maintaining the prison system. This is one of the problems we have not yet solved.

Punishment serves no purpose within the family, except for the temporary relief it gives to the parent who dishes it out. Our objective is to teach the child appropriate behavior, that is, the kind of behavior that contributes to the welfare of the entire family as well as to the welfare of the individual, and helps the young person to become an effective, contributing member of the larger community. This is a long range job, not to be accomplished in an emotional moment. It requires a diligent, steady commitment to the task.

We want our children to learn to conduct themselves in such a way that they will be able to reap life's rewards and help others as well. They have to learn to take care of themselves, to protect themselves from hazards, relate well to others, and contribute to the harmony of the family and of other groups of which they become members.

Examining those objectives, it is clear that punishment for the sake of retribution does not make sense. Many parents, inflicting punishment such as spanking, say or think, "This hurts me more than it does you." That idea stems from the conviction that a parent must do something drastic as a result of misbehavior, and inflicting physical slaps often comes first to mind. The parent who is quick to anger is also likely to be quick to hit and then quick to apologize. The parent who says "This hurts me" has the mistaken idea that inflicting punishment is obligatory, that it is a parental duty for the sake of the child. Such a parent may also say or think, "I'm doing it for your own good" and may believe that. There are better ways. A more effective way is to allow the natural consequences of the misbehavior to reach the child, to let the situation itself affect what happens to the child. This is to call attention to reality rather than retribution.

Another mistaken concept in connection with misbehavior and punishment is that a child must obey the parent. The implication in a superior giving orders to an inferior is precisely contrary to the development of a child towards independence. We want our children to learn to control themselves and to understand how to cooperate with others so that they will function autonomously but in harmony. If they grow up relying on the direction and orders of parents, there is less opportunity for them to learn to make their own decisions, learn from their own mistakes, and develop their own self-discipline.

Children want to manage their own affairs, to have

an opinion about and a chance to direct their own lives. Since this is what a mature adult does, they need to learn while they're young under the example and instruction of parents. Such instruction is not necessarily verbal, but demonstrated far more successfully through activities than words. "Don't do as I do, do as I say" doesn't work and never has worked. But when children actually live through the consequences of their own actions, they learn appropriate behavior and self-control.

Discipline is often confused with punishment. Every child needs discipline; it implies order, structure, and training. We want our youngsters to learn how to approach a task of any kind, doing or learning, in such a way that they can bring it to a satisfactory completion. Such a task might be as simple, for a small child, as putting away the toys, or as complicated, for a teen, as writing a term paper for school. Self-discipline is closely linked to independence as well as to self-confidence. A person's beliefs about herself or himself largely determine the manner of coping with tasks and with life.

For many generations we all believed in the autocratic system in which someone at the top gave orders, enforced them or had them enforced, and the underlings complied. There was a "great chain of being" to illustrate the rankings. Countries operated that way and so did families. Children were expected if seen not to be heard. It was assumed that the head of the house, a male, would rule and all others would bow down, just as with a king and his subjects. However, people's revolutions all over the world, including the American revolution, have brought about the downfall of such systems, so that autocracy doesn't work well any more. Nobody wants to take orders any more: not slaves or serfs, not women or children. In the family, an authoritarian system may work when the children are very young and see no alternate to compliance, but especially in recent years many parents have been faced with the evidence of youth rebellion. Those young people who were compliant when they were small became disorderly as they grew up. We're faced with the challenge to find new ways to live with children as if they are equal human beings, in an atmosphere of cooperation instead of authority.

In *A Parents' Guide to Child Discipline*, (New York: Hawthorn, 1970) Rudolf Dreikurs, M. D., and Loren Grey, Ph. D., say of punishment:

The only children who respond well to punishment are those who do not need it. . . . Those whom we try to impress with punitive consequences may respond briefly, and then resume their defiance. They feel that if the adult has the right to punish, they have the same right too. Mutual retaliations fill our homes and schools. . . one cannot hope for good results through punishment. It has to be replaced by the application of logical or natural consequences where the child is impressed with the needs of reality, not with the power of adults.

When parents don't know what else to do, they mete out punishment. A child commits some act, or fails to perform one, against the parents' intent. The conscientious parent feels that this cannot pass unmarked, and often in anger imposes a sentence of deprivation, isolation, lectures and/or physical attack.

For example Chad, age eight, dawdled when he was supposed to be getting ready to go on an outing with his parents, brother, and sisters. His father called him many times, each time his voice rising. The rest of the family was already in the car when Chad's father lost what remained of his patience. He ran into the house, grabbed Chad by the collar of his shirt, and forcefully shoved him into the car. That was clearly a physical attack, possible only because Chad is still smaller than his father. The result was an angry father, a sullen boy, and an outing that was supposed to be fun for the family was spoiled for everybody.

What Chad's father could have done was to leave without him. That would be the natural consequence of Chad's failure to be ready on time, and Chad would learn that he could not use his power over others. True, the outing might have been curtailed because Chad could not long be left alone, but it was spoiled anyway. At least a helpful lesson would have been taught. Before getting ready, all members of the family could have agreed on what time they would leave. Then, without getting angry, parents follow through with whoever is ready. Next time everybody would be ready on time. The way it was handled, Chad's father later felt remorse for the way he manhandled Chad, his son continued to feel resentful and to think of revenge, and the other children were frightened.

Consider Mimi, age five, who left her toy truck on the stairs of her house leading up to the second floor. She knew that was a dangerous spot and could cause an accident to happen to others in the family, but when her mother called her attention to it Mimi insisted the truck had to stay there. After a few commands to remove it, Mimi's mother yelled at her, spanked her bottom, and sent her to her room. Within a few moments, overcome with the severity of what she had done, she went up to tell her she'd been too harsh, to hug her and to invite her to rejoin the family.

In that response were included the four common elements of punishment: deprivation, isolation, vocal and physical attack. Mimi learned that her mother has power over her while she's small, and that she's not consistent. She discovered that leaving her truck on the stairs creates a big commotion with only a minor inconvenience to herself. Next time she felt bored she might leave a toy there just to see what excitement it would cause.

A more effective response for either of Mimi's parents, after once calling the truck to her attention, would be to remove it promptly from the stairs and put it away in a place where Mimi couldn't get it for a few days or a week. She would thus learn about order and consistency and the logical consequences of misbehavior. If she left a toy in a hazardous spot, it would be removed by others if not by her. She could thereafter decide for herself to keep her toys in the proper place. No commotion would be caused and no excitement would ensue in this recommended procedure. It could be done quietly without fuss, without waiting for escalating anger. Nobody would be displaying power over anybody else. Mimi would not be touched. Safety would be preserved.

Whenever a child acts in such a way as to provoke your parental response, consider the impact of what you are about to do. If you can't count to the recommended ten, count to five, or even three. Instead of a spontaneous retort, think about the effect you will create and endeavor to make it productive of improvement.

Misbehavior usually produces conflict. Sometimes the conflict is between two siblings, and a parent is called upon to settle it. This is one of the worst traps that children set for parents, even if they don't realize it and don't do it intentionally. It's impossible for anybody to decide justly which one has misbehaved and what is a proper penalty. One or the other is sure to say, "That isn't fair." The most effective way to solve a conflict between a sister and brother, or two sisters, or two brothers, or among more, is to stay out of it—completely—and allow them to handle it themselves.

Parents to whom I have given this advice almost always protest "But she'll choke him!" or "He'll bash his head in!" They want to know how long to wait before they intervene, insisting that bodily harm will be done if they don't. This doesn't happen in a normal family. What does happen is that the children discover they cannot pull parents into their squabbles and so the conflicts diminish. Such quarrels, although they are genuine, have as their basic purpose the manipulation of parents. In seeking attention from and power over their parents, children will use any methods. To pick a fight with your brother or sister over a minor matter such as which television show to watch or which chair to sit in is a proven way to get parents stirred up. If things are too quiet around the house, it's fun to create a little action that way. Then the participants accomplish two things: they gain the parents' attention and disturb whatever the parents were doing. If you don't fall for their tricks, there's no fun left in the squabbles.

To test this, tell your children that you have decided that they are able to handle their own differences and that from now on you will trust them to do so. If a very young infant (under a year, not able to move out of the way) is around, you may have to protect the baby by removing him or her from the battleground, but let the others alone. If you deliberately and completely keep quiet and stay away, within a short time the fights between and among the children will diminish.

This does not mean there will never be sibling rivalry. Conflict is inevitable when people live together, and it is likely that there will be disagreements. But they will be much less violent, much less noisy, and much shorter if the children know they can't drag their parents into their fights. To avoid the damage done by intense competition between siblings, do not compare them to one another at any time in any way. Such comparisons only serve to discourage the one who is considered less competent, less reliable, less orderly, or less successful. Discouragement doesn't produce improvement; it produces defeat. When you judge who's "right" to settle an argument, you are usually proclaiming a winner and a loser. It's impossible always to be fair, so don't try.

In our society we live by the clock, and thus one of the irritations that besets parents is children's failure to be on time, as noted above in the example of Chad. They don't come in for meals, or they don't go to bed when they're supposed to, or they're not ready for school in the morning. When children play outdoors or are engaged in some absorbing occupation, they don't want to stop the first time they're called and often lead their mothers and/or fathers to exasperation before they finally come. One child was even heard to say, "She's not yelling yet!" when asked why he didn't respond to his mother's call. He was accustomed to waiting for her anger. The way to retrain a child from such an expectation is to go ahead without him or her, without anger.

On the subject of being called, if your children have the annoying habit of calling to you from another room, the best way to cure it is not to respond. State that you will not answer a shout, and then don't. When the child discovers that you will neither answer nor come, she or he will come to you. Of course you can tell when there is a real emergency, and in that event, you will run. But in everyday life people can go toward another person to speak instead of yelling from a distance.

Another source of irritation is getting up in the morning. Parents expend energy trying to awaken the reluctant child and then get her or him washed, fed, and dressed to be ready for the day. In community centers I listen to parents talking at their children, and the most used phrase is "Hurry up!" It's said automatically every few minutes as the child dresses or undresses, and probably used just as often at home too. Saying "Hurry up!" doesn't make anybody hurry. All it does is tell the child that the parent is impatient. This may work to slow the youngster down, for there can be great satisfaction in prolonging mother's or father's distress.

The way to teach children about the value of promptness is to establish a routine (of course being on time yourself) and then expect them to abide by it. People who are always late are the ones who want to keep other people waiting—it is a way of exerting their dominance over them. Consider how you feel about an adult friend who comes late to everything. No matter how much you like that person, if you're reasonably prompt, you resent having to wait. Good excuses don't help much, either.

To create promptness, allow children to decide when they will do what (they do decide anyway) and then let them absorb the consequences of their decision. For instance, when it is time to come in for a meal, call the child once. If he or she does not arrive promptly, begin the meal without him or her. Then allow no snacks nor substitutes; the child waits for the next regular meal time.

This assumes that meals are available in your home at regularly agreed hours. You will of course explain in advance what you are going to do so that the child understands a new system is beginning. But do not wait until you are upset or angry to do anything about it and do not give lectures to emphasize what you're doing. Just take action instead of saying words. The only way natural consequences work is if they occur in a calm orderly atmosphere.

For getting up in the morning, one call will suffice if the child knows there will be no more. By the age of five or six each child can have her or his own alarm clock, set it and arise by it. Assume that the child will get up and get ready on time. Practice trust. Proceed with your own morning routine without reminders to the child. You may be inconvenienced by the first two or three attempts, but choose a time when you can bear such an inconvenience. Leave it to the child to be ready, and let the consequences follow. Some mothers have taken or sent a child to school incompletely dressed; others have allowed the child to be tardy. The consequence has to fit the situation, but haranguing is not training. Retraining towards self-reliance is what is needed for the child who expects others to serve her or him.

Let the child choose what to wear, thus eliminating one more opportunity for conflict. If the youngster does need help with tying shoes for instance, wait to be asked. Allow sufficient time so that the young one can do for himself or herself what you could do faster. Many little children give up trying to dress themselves, or wash themselves, when a parent takes over. Surely you could do it faster and better, but the child has to learn. Don't expect perfection. A smudge isn't as important as the child's growing competence.

There are as many kinds of misbehavior as there are families. Another of the commonest is that a child makes a mess; it may be in the kitchen, the bathroom, or any room in the house. The circumstances may be fixing a snack, tracking in mud, wetting or soiling, or merely routine play. The best consequence is for the child to clean up the mess. The way to enforce it is not by yelling, screaming, or hitting, but by expecting the child to undo the damage, to clean up and/or put away. You may have to hold other activities in abeyance waiting until the job is done, and you may have to lower perfectionistic standards so that the child can do the job. You may even have to help a little, but the responsibility is to be the child's. If more than one child was involved, they join in the cleanup as they did in the act.

This is not permissiveness. Permissiveness says "Let them alone so they won't get frustrated. Don't hamper their tender psyches." But children need to learn limits. If parents back off and let them do whatever they want whenever they want, only chaos and confusion results. Not too long ago it was widely believed and advised by professionals that "if you love them enough, they'll come out all right." That is not necessarily true, as many parents have discovered in recent years. It's a stock phrase concocted when you can't figure out what else to say and may have been accurate in times past. When families were headed by an autocrat who could issue decrees and enforce them, it wasn't necessary for parents to learn how to get along with their children. Families lived as did many generations before them. Parents ordered and children obeyed. Fathers usually issued the decrees, mothers carried them out, often waiting for father to reappear to administer punishment. Children who didn't obey were "bad." Autocracy doesn't work any more and parents have to learn to live with their children in a democratic atmosphere in which children speak up and participate in decisions about their own lives.

Each child decides for herself what to do, when to do it, and how to behave. Early behavior is based on the perceptions a child makes in reaction to others, especially parents. When parents change the way they speak and act with their children, the children respond with changed behavior. Before improvement comes, however, there may be an intensification of the poor behavior, for the children will test to find out whether the new way is permanent or just another passing whim.

What upsets parents most about children's misbehavior is not just the acts, but the ensuing arguments. Mothers and fathers typically talk endlessly, hoping that the sheer force of repetition will accomplish correction. It doesn't. What parents think of as "reasoning" children often call "lectures" and pay no attention. They turn off their hearing. Parents need to change their emphasis from talking to acting. Instead of scolding, take action in the situation and have greater impact.

What can you do if your spouse doesn't agree with you? Maybe you're convinced that you want to change the way things are handled in your house, to do what is suggested here, but you can't persuade your husband or wife. Of course it would be better if you could act together, but you don't have to hesitate. Choose one aspect of the activities in your family that you'd like to change, and then go ahead alone. You can have a profound effect on the behavior of one child, or all the children, even if you're the only one who stops shouting and takes action. Your spouse will be affected too. Don't try to do it all at once, but select some one thing that seems feasible to you to do, and then work on that. When that succeeds, you can add another. Meanwhile, the evidence will show your spouse that the new way works, and it may be persuasive enough so that he or she will join with you.

Parents worry about raising their children to be good citizens, and with every misdemeanor they fear the worst. It's far better to take prompt action so that the child can learn rather than to wring one's hands, shed one's tears, and exaggerate the importance of a single misstep. But don't expect to recreate the world in a day. Allow yourself—and the children—time to practice fresh approaches. Learn to notice small improvements so that you encourage yourself as well as the other family members.

Children need attention, guidance, instruction, and love from their parents, and if they get them on a continuing basis, they are less likely to provoke their parents by poor behavior. Pay attention to them at times other than the conflict-laden periods, and they will have less impetus to manipulate you by naughtiness. Set aside a private time for each child every day, even if it is only for ten or fifteen minutes, so that your undivided attention is devoted to one son or daughter. Let the child decide how it is to be used: play a game, read a story, or just talk together. Children will admit that the spanking or other punishment they get is worthwhile, for at least when they get it they know the parent is paying attention. It is sometimes better, in the child's mind, to get hurt than to be ignored. When parents ignore destructive behavior and notice constructive behavior, their children respond. Likewise, if parents pay attention voluntarily with pleasure, their children don't have to misbehave to get their notice.

A broad principle to keep in mind when attempting to alter children's behavior is that children respond best to those acts and words that they perceive as encouraging, and worst to punishment and degrading comments, which inflict discouragement. Encouragement enables, discouragement disables.

chapter nine

The Value of Cooperation

The person who is so independent as to be unable to cooperate with others will not find a comfortable place in the world. Such a person is not adequately prepared for living in a society of humans, for we are all interdependent. Each of us depends to some extent on the performance of others, from the caretakers of our public utilities to the producers of the goods we consume. Even in this time of automation, countless individuals perform their duties for the benefit of all of us, and we can hardly grasp the scope of our mutual need. Occasionally when an interruption occurs in our systems we realize how much we lean on one another, but most of the time we take for granted the contributions of others toward us and ours toward them.

Furthermore, it is as necessary to feel like a part of a group as it is to feel confidence in one's self, for we are continually a part of a circle of others, not always of our own choosing. Distorted emphasis on "adjustment" to the world has made it seem as though we have only two choices: to train our children to be independent, or to bring them up with so few limits that they adapt to anything. On the contrary, the independent person is better able to get along with others, for that person has a solid foundation of self-esteem from which to build. With that, it is easier to cooperate.

How do we help our children learn to cooperate at the same time we are teaching them to be independent? First, by creating a cooperative atmosphere in the family. This may mean examining your own role as a parent, and questioning it. It is almost impossible to maintain authority and expect willing cooperation. The goal is, "We're all in this together." In such a setting each member treats every other member with respect, there is mutual trust, and every person has intrinsic value. Some are bigger, stronger, know more. The younger ones are dependent on their elders for sustenance and guidance, and the innate talents differ in each person. But in such a family, people are treated as if they are equal to each other in human worth. In fact, no one can accurately measure the comparative value of human beings; our religions teach us that only a deity can make that kind of decision.

Part of the reluctance of parents to train their children to be independent stems from the fear that this will make them "selfish," exclusively self-centered. No one wants to raise an arrogant child, one who is concerned only for herself or himself. Fathers and mothers feel further threatened by the possibility that their children will not need them; that they will grow away from them and care only for themselves. Parents don't want to be cast off by their children, nor do they want them to be cold and/or cruel to other people. Therefore, the thrust for independence is best combined with an example of and consideration for cooperation. Within the family, where affection and concern have their best source of nutrition, cooperation is not only advisable but absolutely essential to the conduct of harmonious family life. Since affection and concern are most easily cultivated in the family, this is a good beginning to instill the kind of consideration for one another that cooperation implies.

When parents assume full responsibility for the family, treating their children as subordinates to be sheltered from life's burdens, they deprive the children of chances to learn how to cooperate with other people on a daily basis. If the family is governed in a system in which parents have the authority because they are superior, the children are likely to feel forever inferior and not make the optimum growth that will lead them to be fully functioning adults.

The tragedy is that one or both parents may feel inferior herself or himself, having grown up under conditions that led to such a view. On becoming parents, they may attempt to assert their own significance by dominating their children. Thus are the errors of one generation passed on to the next. But it is possible to break that transmission in a way that everyone in the family gains.

Children, given the chance, will respond with refreshing shifts in behavior and communication. When they are treated with respect, they give respect. When they are trusted, they become trustworthy. When their point of view is respected and they are allowed to share in making decisions that affect them, they will conduct themselves according to those decisions. They are not marionettes on strings to be controlled by a master operator, as many parents discover in the very first weeks of a baby's life. Although they know this, mothers and fathers sometimes go on assuming that they can control their children and shape them any way they want. Much family conflict arises as a result of such misunderstanding. Parents truly believe that they can tell their children what to do, and the children will do it. Children just as strongly feel that they can do whatever they want, and they go ahead and do it.

Children are susceptible to their parents' behavior and react according to their ideas of how they can hold on to their importance. Each of us, adults and children alike, has a pattern of life to help us gain significance. We act in certain ways and say certain things in order to maintain our place in the world. Some of our behavior is based on false assumptions, but we don't always discover they are false. As adults, we continue to believe that we are inadequate, or inferior, and must compensate in other ways for what we perceive to be our weaknesses. We suffer from our chronic human imperfection, feeling that we're not good enough.

Regardless of whether we parents change our ideas about ourselves, when we change our attitudes, acts, and communication with our children, the children can change their ideas about themselves, as well as their behavior. A common example is the child who is constantly occupied in strategies to keep his mother busy paying attention. When mother stops responding to the demands for attention and instead pays attention to him willingly at times when she is not annoyed, the child's behavior changes. The demands for attention disappear. The effort the child had been putting forth in keeping his mother busy can be directed toward more productive activity.

Each of us strives to be significant among others, in the world as well as in the family. When children leave home they meet a group of new people who do not necessarily treat them as they have been treated at home. Those who have not grown in a cooperative system will not know how to cooperate. They will attempt to fit into other groups without quite knowing how, and may falter and fail. They may feel continually inadequate, somehow inferior, and always like an outsider. But those who have learned at home how to carry their share of responsibility and to cooperate are better prepared to share in the work or play of others. Those who have learned at home to listen to other people as well as to express themselves are better prepared to engage in the kind of effective communication that makes rewarding human relationships.

One of the best ways to enhance cooperation within the family among all members is the family council. In it parents as well as children learn to listen to each other and really hear what is being said, to express themselves without fear of reprisal, and jointly to cope with the family's problems.

This is how it's done.

On a regularly scheduled basis all members of the family gather at a prearranged time and place. Everybody who lives together, sharing the home, whether or not they are related, is included. Usually this means parents and children, but anybody who is staying more than a week, such as a grandmother, a cousin, or a friend, would join in.

One person, not necessarily a parent or adult, leads the discussion. The choice of who will preside rotates among all members of the family capable of speech, so that everybody, including children, has a chance to act as leader. If there is an infant who does not yet speak well, he or she is included in the meeting to learn by listening. The person who keeps order, leading the group, may be called the chairperson, the leader, the monitor, or any title that suits the family. Usually another person keeps a record of decisions made and agreements reached. This role also rotates, and may be called the secretary, the scribe, the recorder, or by any other suitable name.

Paramount is the requirement that whatever anybody says during the meeting, no punishment will follow. In the excitement of free expression, it is almost inevitable that remarks will be made that might be inflammatory. Regardless of what is the usual procedure when such words are uttered, no attempt is to be made to stifle them or to punish the person who made them. Doing so will thwart the purpose of the meeting. If such remarks are allowed to escape, this may clear the air for finding the source of conflict. Then the conflict can be solved. The family council is a specific time set aside for a specific purpose, and those who participate agree that there will be free and open discussion of the activities and relationships within and affecting the family, so that all who attend can share in making decisions.

The agenda is determined by what happens in the family and what difficulties its members have. One way to get things on the agenda is to post a memo in a handy place. Anyone who wants something brought up at the family meeting writes it on that memo, and when meeting time comes around, the agenda is ready. Preparing such a list in advance can take the fire out of situations that occur between meetings. Once a subject is on the agenda, it waits to be handled at the meeting. Emphasis for the topic is on the situation, not on the individual. The question for the family council is "How can we get the garbage out on time?" not "How can we make Johnny take out the garbage?"

If making a list in advance is too much bother, the agenda can be prepared as the session begins. Any aspects of family life are opened for discussion. Meeting time is not the time to discuss political events or the weather, unless such topics have direct relevance to family affairs. Nor is it the time to bring up old hurts and old grievances. Family council is for talking together about what is going on today and this week in the family and how best to work together cooperatively to make family life more satisfying for all the members.

Having a set time every week accomplishes several purposes. When everybody knows the meeting is coming, conflicts are held in abeyance until that time, to be opened and solved when the heat has cooled. Since everyone knows in advance when the meeting is to be, they can arrange their other commitments so as to be present. Otherwise decisions may be made without their input. The whole family gets used to gathering at that time, and the council meeting becomes a main event in the maintenance of family ties.

An error that spoils many family meetings is to use them merely as gripe sessions. Every member has a complaint against someone else, but if emphasis is in that direction, nobody wants to come. Sessions need to include what's good about family life, too, and what's good about every member. In fact, it is conducive to full participation to start and end with such comments of encouragement. Just as nobody wants to listen to nothing but gripes, everybody wants to hear something good about themselves.

The chairperson can start the meeting with a comment on something about the family that she or he feels good about at the moment, and then ask each one in attendance to report one good thing about the family. These comments may apply to one family member, or more, as well as to the family as a whole. The meeting then proceeds to any problems that are ripe for consideration, and the meeting finishes on another encouraging note. Before adjournment, the chairman asks for suggestions for family fun later, so that all cooperate in the enjoyment as well as in the responsibilities. The fun planned for later can be as simple as playing a game together or as involved as planning a trip somewhere. The younger the children, the more important it is that the fun come promptly. A treat to eat, either at home or out, is a start, if the meeting follows a meal. Other possibilities are to play a game together, indoors or out, go for a walk, or a bike ride, make or listen to music that all can enjoy.

In every household there are chores that must be done to supply the practical needs of life. Food has to be purchased, brought in, put away, prepared. After that's done there are dishes to wash and a kitchen to clean. Clothes have to be provided and made clean after they are worn. If there is a family pet, it needs a routine of care. According to the season, there may be a lawn to mow or snow to remove. When parents assign such jobs, they usually meet resistance and create dissension. The scene in which a parent calls a child to come and do the dishes, take out the garbage, walk the dog, or bring up the laundry often ends in an angry parent and a resentful child. It is repeated over and over in every household, but not always with the result that the job gets done. Often the parent does it to avoid the frustration of trying to get someone else to do it. It seems simpler that way. And quieter.

When parents assign chores, children are usually unwilling to perform them, and if they do so, it is under duress. When children are instead included in the consideration of what needs to be done and how the jobs are to get done, they are much more willing to do their share. Prepare a list of all the tasks of the household, and at the meeting ask the family members to choose which ones they will assume. You may be surprised when a boy asks to clear the table or a girl to shovel snow. Let them find out what it's like to do different things than the tasks they have previously been assigned to do. Record the choices with the understanding that the decision holds for the week, until the next meeting. At that time changes can be made. Issue no reminders throughout the week, and do not intrude in the performance of the jobs. Of course the children's standards of performance may not be the same as the parents', or their ability may not yet be at the level of the parents', but they will learn thus to cooperate in the functioning of the family.

They will not learn to cooperate if they are given orders. They may learn to obey orders, but this is not conducive to independent thought or action. It leads to resentment and sometimes to rebellion. What parents call "laziness" may be the child's way of showing the parent "You can't make me!" Big family fights happen when the parent feels "Oh yes I can!"

A shift from assigning chores to sharing them among family members can diminish the noise level, the anger, and the resentment. No one has to serve anybody else, but all cooperate.

It may seem easier for one adult, or both adults, to decide what the children should do and then issue the orders, but the extra effort it takes to establish cooperation is rewarded by the change in the family and in the children. Another dividend is that the children learn at an early age that they are not guests on the earth to be served, but that they can contribute to their own well-being as well as to the welfare of the family and the world.

The family council that is successful and teaches everybody how to cooperate meets these criteria: regular meetings at a prearranged time; open discussion; rules of operation accepted by all; no recriminations afterward; respect for each other; opportunity for all to participate, both in deliberations and in decisions. There is also the agreement that decisions made at one meeting are valid until the next meeting, at which time they can be reconsidered.

To realize the value of such a system, think of the relationships between and among the people in it. Each one connects to one other, in what professionals call a "dyad," a couple, a pair. But within such a pair there are differences of opinion, alternatives in approach, and variations in points of view as well as affection and caring. In a family that includes more than two persons, as families usually do, the number of variations in opinions, approaches, points of view, and levels of affection increases in many directions. There are not only additional dyads within the family, but trios and quartets as well, sometimes to the exclusion of one person. Most of us grew up in families, and we need only reflect on the composition of our own to recall the alliances and enmities of family life. Such alliances sometimes last throughout our lifetime, but they may change from time to time depending on the situation.

The family that meets regularly in family council is in less danger of competitive rivalry that splits it into factions. There will be combinations of members, but their energy is more likely to be directed toward the welfare of the family as a whole than toward individual superiority.

The first alliance, of course, is the parents. If you want to build a cooperative family, it is helpful to have such an alliance, a basis of trust between mother and father, but it is not to be used against the children. This is a common mistake: to view family life as "us" vs. "them." It's not a contest to see who's going to win, but rather a venture in which each succeeding person who joins the family becomes a partner in the pursuit of the general welfare.

Children will ally with one another against the parents if they see this as the theme of family life. Family council helps to prevent this. Parents can also guard against hostility between the children if they deliberately refrain from comparing them with one another. The trouble with comparisons is that one child is held up as somehow better than the other, which results in the other one feeling put down. Such comparisons do not inspire, they discourage.

Another way to avoid developing rancor between children is not to accept tattling on each other at any time, neither in daily life nor in the family council. Just as in sibling squabbles, parents are most effective when they refuse to become embroiled in the reports of witnesses to an alleged misdeed. Let them know that you believe they can handle the situation.

Unlike a governmental council, the family council does not vote to see who wins. Decisions are made by total agreement. If unanimous agreement cannot be reached, the subject is tabled for the next meeting. Making decisions by the weight of votes is apt to set up the very competition that family council seeks to avoid. A vote may be taken on a simple choice, such as which restaurant or which museum to visit. But avoid taking votes on vital matters that will affect the losers as well as the winners.

Every family has its own strengths, and following the general guidelines, each family can work out its own cooperative system, adapting the family council to suit its needs. If your goal is clear that you want your children to become independent and cooperative, you can create a framework that will help them develop in that direction. You will have to abdicate your absolute authority and create instead an atmosphere of joint effort.

chapter ten

Money and Financial Responsibility

Devoted as parents are to the idea that their children should become independent, the reality of life is that children are financially dependent on others for a very long period of time. As described in Chapter Two, child life in our society requires financial, as well as physical and emotional support for about two decades. Recent estimates of what it costs to raise a child from birth to adulthood range in the hundreds of thousands of dollars, depending on what is included in the figures.

Human beings not only reach maturity later than other mammals, but require much more elaborate training and education for adult life. This consumes a large part of the financial assets of the human community and specifically of an individual's parents. In addition, parents provide shelter, food, clothing, and amusements. Added together, this puts a heavy burden on the parent that can become a hindrance to the development of healthy relationships between the generations.

A mother once asked me, "What about accountability?" Her question was meant to show that a child must be accountable for the money parents spend on him or her.

She was thinking in terms of a balance sheet, with debits and credits. That kind of bookkeeping can lead only to mutual hostility. You can't very well fire your children if they don't pay up. Or if they're not satisfactory, you can't trade them in for others. Parenthood isn't the kind of enterprise one begins with the expectation of making a profit. You can't treat your children as a business operation if you expect them to become fully human. If you want to raise people you can't treat them like things.

What is money anyway? A brief definition would say it is something issued by a recognized authority, used as a medium of exchange for something of value. That's all it is—a medium of exchange for something else. Its value lies only in what you can do with it. But it's a symbol interpreted in many ways. We measure ourselves and others by how much or how little money we have and how important it is to us. Since we don't wear it on our persons as wampum, we want to own the things it buys, trying to prove to ourselves and others that we have intrinsic value. We choose many of our entertainments and activities just to prove we can afford them. Likewise, we crave more and better possessions to show even ourselves that we are able to get them. Of course, we don't consciously think about what we're trying to prove when we join the club, buy the car, or get the coat, but the symbolism underlies the expense, just the same.

We don't often think of money in terms of what it represents. We're all much more accustomed to thinking of whether we have enough, and how to get more. But in our lives with our children we are teaching them about money whether we intend to or not. They watch what we buy with it, they listen to what we say about it, and they absorb our value system. They may argue with us about money, but in order to do so they first have received messages from us that tell them how we feel about money and possessions.

Money is the basic tool for survival in an industrial society such as ours. Literally, without money one can die. With it, one can buy the necessities of life and survive. This leads to money itself becoming a primary goal, instead of being used merely as a tool to get what we want out of life. If we don't know what we really want, we're more apt to expect money to be the answer.

Each parent treats money and possessions according to a private system of beliefs and will use it with children within the framework of those beliefs. To some parents, a comfortable home is most important; funds are spent to buy such a home, or rent it, and to furnish and equip it. To other parents, education is highest on the priority list; funds are spent for what the parents perceive as the best possible educational opportunities. To some it is most important to put up a good front, so money is spent first for clothes, cars, and things that show. Others are concerned that their children enjoy themselves, so they buy toys, games, and equipment, while still others are confronted with decisions about orthodontics or orthopedics. In the absence of clear priorities, parents can feel like tumbleweed tossed in the wind, blown in the direction of any gust of want.

We usually imagine that everybody has the same priorities we do, or at least that our relatives, close friends and neighbors do. But a careful view of how others spend and/or save will show that everybody has his own ideas about money. What we do with it expresses those ideas more than what we say. In a period of rising inflation, money assumes even greater importance and becomes a subject of universal concern. Children are aware of its effects too, so they can be taken into your confidence when their wishes exceed your treasury.

No parent is immune from the worry and the resentment that arises from the necessity to be continually giving. Parenthood is often described just that way: one long process of parents giving and children taking, not only money but time and labor. One of the dangers inherent in the transactions is that parents may feel entitled to get love, appreciation, and/or respect mainly on the basis of their financial investment and the work that is required to earn the family income. After all, it is fathers and mothers who go out into the world to earn the bread the children eat. They can't be blamed for wanting appreciation. Even those whose income comes without labor, as when it is inherited, are not immune from similar feelings. Parents have to give, but children don't always give back. That's another reason to think carefully about how you want to allot your money, and what is really important to the family well-being.

There are many variations on parental attitudes and expectations toward money and gifts. They range from the stingy parent who gives as little as possible, expecting ingratitude, to the generous one who buys and buys, hoping to get love and approval in return. Both of these extremes illustrate destructive ways of attaching undue importance to money and gifts as signs of love. In the vast middle are all the rest of us who struggle along meeting our obligations, providing necessities for our children and occasional treats, and wondering what kind of money management we are teaching.

Problems arise not with supplying the necessities, but in deciding what is actually necessary and what they can get along without; that is, using discretion. We know we have to feed our children, but we're not sure whether we must take them out to eat. We know we have to clothe them, but we're not sure whether we must buy the latest fad garment that their friends are said to be wearing. If you find yourself resenting the money that you spend on your children that isn't absolutely necessary, stop. It's better to say, "We're spending too much on trips and treats. We're cutting down" and then to do it, rather than continue to lay out the money. Some parents, believing for instance that summer camp is good for their children, may even borrow to make it possible, and then carry a seething resentment against the child for whom the obligation was incurred. Nobody likes martyrs, and children would much rather be deprived of something than have to listen to speeches about "All I've done for you." Another incident of this kind occurs when parents pay for lessons in which a child then loses interest. Either do it freely, or if you can't afford it, don't do it. If you first spend the money and then harangue the child, you've just added conflict to family life. Rather than learning the value of money, the child may only learn how to provoke a parent in a painful way.

To raise them to be independent, we are concerned that our children learn to handle money and to use it well. We want them to know how to function in the world that includes the market place. No matter what our own system of values is, we want our children to form an individual appreciation of the value of money—how to get it and how to use it responsibly. While they are dependent on us they need to learn so that they are prepared for their later independence. The parent who bestows money and gifts without plan and/or without limits during the child's dependent years will meet an adult son or daughter who can't manage life's financial responsibilities. Especially in times of easy credit, many young people sign up for everything they want as soon as they have a job, only to find out that they can't pay for it all. Managing money requires training and experience.

For financial training to make sense, parents must first arrive at a clear understanding of their own goals. Are you trying to save your money against an uncertain future, putting away every extra dollar, or do you want to keep up with your neighbors, getting every new thing that appears on the market? You can't do both. Do you have large amounts of discretionary income, money that isn't required to pay your basic expenses, or are you struggling to meet your bills? Both situations present dilemmas. Is the amount of money you earn the most important thing about your job, or are you more interested in enjoying what you do? Both have to be balanced. Do both parents agree on how money should be managed? Spend some time talking about your goals so that you can know your priorities.

If you want your child to learn to handle money well, the earlier he or she starts, the better. The only way to learn the basic skills of money management is by practice, by making mistakes and learning from them. That is the rationale for an allowance to be given to a child on a regular basis as early as possible, probably at around age five.

A child at that age is just learning the difference in the size and monetary value of coins and what they will buy. The allowance is a share of the family's discretionary income, to be allotted freely with no strings attached. Parents do not control how it is spent. They merely an-

swer questions and supply information. They do not prescribe how, when or on what the money is to be used.
The amount is small enough so that even if it is spent
foolishly there is no great loss. In these inflationary times,
one cannot specify how much it should be; what a dime
buys today as this is written may need a quarter by the
time it is in print. But it should be a single coin of small
denomination, so that the child can hold it, own it, and
learn to understand its use.

As the child grows older, the allowance gets larger, but
at no time is it to be tied in any way to punishment or
failure to perform responsibilities. The practice in many
families to threaten or actually withhold money from children doesn't work to correct behavior. It only prolongs
conflict, putting parents in the position of judges impos-
ing fines. There is no connection between school grades
and allowance either; giving or taking away money for
such a reason only leads the child to distorted values. If
you give money for good grades, or take it away for bad
grades, you are saying to the child that she or he is to
make an effort only if they get paid. The emphasis of
school is, or ought to be, on learning as preparation for
life. Grades may or may not be indicative of what a child
is actually learning. Nor does it make any sense to withhold allowance as punishment. The objective of punishment is to improve the child's behavior. Since there is no
connection between money and the incident, this is another ploy that doesn't work.

But what if a child breaks something? Who pays for it?
Before you issue a decree, consider who pays for it when
an adult breaks something. Ponder the difference between
the cost of the broken window if father drives the ball
through it accidentally, or if the accident happens when

his son is at bat. The trouble with requiring a child to pay for a broken object is that the child rarely has enough money, and must mortgage himself for months to come. By the time the debt would be paid off, the impact of the event would long have been forgotten but the deprivation would linger. What actually happens is that after the first fury dies down, the parents forget about it anyway. In the face of such inconsistency, children know how often their parents change their minds, and so they may pay little attention to the pronouncements of penalty.

Thus in this as in other aspects of life, don't act on spontaneous anger but consider the effect of what you are about to impose. Treat the children as responsible members of the family group and they are more likely to act that way. Don't feel sorry for them, or pity them, for that tells them they're puny and helpless. Instead of issuing judgment upon them, ask them to contribute their ideas to how the situation might be remedied. They may surprise you. They will learn better if you are reasonable and consistent than if you impose punitive measures you can't enforce.

In order to plan the amount of allowance, you must first gather figures on which it can be based. Keep a record for a month or more of how much money you actually hand out, and then decide on a proper amount. When children start school you will want to take into consideration their expenses for school supplies, equipment, lunch and bus fares. In the beginning you may not want to include all of this in the allowance but as they grow in responsibility they can take care of greater amounts. Start with an estimate and be open to the proven necessity for a raise. A few weeks after the school year begins, when children enter a new grade, bring up the subject at family meeting to discuss the allowance—how it is being handled, whether it is enough or too much, and how long it is to stay at the current rate. Review the subject several times during the year so there is agreement between parents and children on what the allowance is to cover. If the allowance is to be a successful learning tool, don't hand out any supplementary sums.

Many parents feel that an allowance isn't necessary. "They can just come to me when they need money," one father says. Or another mother says, "I want them to know they have to ask for money. It doesn't grow on trees, and that way I can decide whether they need it." Both attitudes can lead to undue dependence and sometimes to humiliation. The object of giving a child an allowance on a regular basis, with no strings attached and without waiting for the youngster to ask for it is that the child learns to manage money by having some to practice with. This regularity also helps the youngster learn to plan ahead, which is absolutely essential in an economy such as ours. If you want to save up for something, you have to know what income you can count on. Every member of the family needs the privacy of having his own money. If you have to ask for it, it puts you at a disadvantage. Asking for money can make a person feel like a beggar, leading to a humiliating feeling of being inferior. Arranging for a regular allowance makes this unnecessary.

It is just as important to guard against giving handouts in between allowance times. When the child has used up the allowance, that's all there is. Only in that way can she learn that there are limits to what a person can have and to decide how money is to be used. If there's always more where the last money came from, there's no incentive to make careful plans.

When children enter their teens, an allowance to cover their clothing will both teach them another lesson in management and diminish family conflict over what they can have to wear. Reviewing how much money it has taken in the past to outfit one child, decide upon an amount to be made available for clothes and accessories. Of course you have to take into account that this is a period of rapid growth and a shift into a different size range, costing more. Allow the adolescent to make her or his own choices within the agreed sum. When the money runs out, there are no more clothes. In the unlikely event that the clothing allowance has a balance, decide in advance whether it may be used by the teen for other purposes. In your early discussion, agree whether the amount is to cover special outfits for sports, major purchases like winter coats, or garments for special occasions such as confirmations, weddings, and family events. It would be helpful, too, to discuss whether the teen's earnings are to cover any part of it.

As opportunities to earn extra money appear, the family allowance can be reduced to take them into account, but it's a good idea to maintain at least a minimum allowance until the young person is self-supporting. Nobody should be paid for doing jobs in the home unless those are jobs for which the family would hire outside help. In that event, if youngsters want to take on the job, agree in advance on standards of performance and wages to be paid. This applies equally to work such as window washing, wall cleaning, or similar major projects as it does to baby-sitting. One member of the family should not just be assigned to sit for a younger child. This can create unnecessary tension between the siblings. Take up the question of baby sitting at a family meeting as described in Chapter

Nine, and negotiate the rates and conditions in advance.

An older child who takes care of a younger sister or brother is expected to exert the same level of care and responsibility as would a sitter hired from outside the family. If the children are too near the same age for one to be put in charge over the other, they can be equally responsible for each other without payment. Or, if there is a much younger sibling that needs care and supervision, two older ones can share in the responsibility and in the payment for baby-sitting. The way negotiations are handled depends on the particular family circumstances, but the broad guidelines apply.

If when you employ your youngsters they earn a lot of cash, this may cause you concern, both because they will have excess amounts to handle and because you may not find it convenient to pay it out at the time. A good system is to keep a family financial record in which the money earned is noted, and against which children can make later withdrawals for a purpose. Deposits and withdrawals can be entered at a family meeting and discussed there. Thus parents have an opportunity to express their opinions about any purchase a young person intends to make, or explain why they cannot lay out the cash at that moment. Doing the family bookkeeping in this way also introduces children to the necessity for keeping accurate records. They may take their turn at making the entries, thus learning how to keep their own records when they leave home. It's also a good time to teach them how to write checks and how to safeguard the checkbook balance. All such lessons are to be learned at some time, and the child who has had the chance to learn them at home is better prepared for the future.

Parents often complain that children have no respect

for the value of their toys and possessions. This stems from the fact that many children simply have more of everything than they need, can use, or enjoy. We live in an economy devoted to growth of the gross national product, and one of the ways that contemporary life assures ongoing production is to create constant consumption. We are surrounded with advertisements for things so that we want more and are tempted to buy more. More is then produced which is in turn consumed. In a simpler time and place we could certainly get along without a pulsating shower head or an electric potato peeler, but they or products like them make our adult lives more pleasant.

Our children, however, are growing and developing, forming their ideas about themselves and the world, and need to stretch their imaginations and use their creativity as they grow. Not only do they not need infinite variations on games and toys, but they are actually better off without many of them. Toys help children learn if in the use of them they have to participate: to think, to dream, to plan, to act. There may be temporary amusement in watching something perform by itself, but if there is no activity connected with it, the object becomes merely another piece of clutter on the floor.

Virginia Knauer, consumer consultant, said, "Parents have a responsibility to teach children how to use and take care of their toys." She went on to say that parents ought to provide a specific place for toys to be kept and then arrange to put away, out of reach of the child, duplicates and superfluous ones (*Chicago Tribune*, December 5, 1978).

Many homes, or rooms in them, are in a continual state of disorder because children have so much stuff they can't keep up with it. They pick up one thing, tire of it promptly and leave it where it fell. There are enough toys to keep doing this all day, with the result that nothing is really enjoyed and it all makes a mess. If such disorder doesn't bother you, you're in a minority, and you may ignore my comments. But if it does, start early to teach your child where toys are to be kept, and how to get them there. Don't expect a toddler to put things away, but on the other hand don't assume that you must do it all. The very young child who has just discovered that it's a good game to empty the container of blocks or puzzle pieces can also be shown that it's a good game to put everything back in. This of course requires that a regular storage place is provided and that someone helps the child learn to do what he or she can to make things neat. If you want your children to appreciate what they have and to take care of it, don't buy much more. It may be harder to resist a child's plea than to buy one more gimmick, but in the long run you'll all be better off. Many of the toys bought because children beg for them lose their appeal as soon as the plastic wrapper is removed. A parent who has spent money for such a gadget at the child's insistence naturally becomes annoyed to see it tossed aside. Then there is additional annoyance when you trip over it. If your funds are unlimited, you may want to buy anything the child's heart desires, but if you're like most parents, you're torn between buying what the child wants and what you can afford. It's never too early to say "no," but in order for this to be effective, you must hold on to it. If the child learns how to wear you down by crying and begging in public, so that you say "yes" after a while, you might as well say "yes" at the beginning. If you really want to be effective, you will decide what to buy and how much to spend, remembering that spending money for things is no substitute for spending time with your child.

The strain on the parent and on the family budget can be alleviated if you refuse to be drawn into the televised commands or the child's whine. The child too will discover that she or he can amuse herself or himself quite well with the things already available. For toddlers, pots and pans to bang are among the best playthings. As children grow, building blocks, trucks, and dolls provide more opportunities for the use of imagination and creative ability than all the powered gadgets that flash and scream. Paper, paints, and crayons in a proper place to use them are more valuable to the child's development than any number of turned-on mechanical marvels. Making things is more productive, and can be cheaper, than collecting things. Look for things the child can do. Instead of providing a toy to keep a child out of your way while you do housework or chores, help the child learn to do it with you. It may take longer, but that way you teach valuable skills and give the child the feeling of participating in a necessary task.

If your child receives many toys or possessions from grandparents, relatives, or others, you cannot exercise control over them. But you can restrain yourself. You can also put away extra stuff so that the child has only as much to play with as she or he can enjoy and care for.

Children don't take care of their clothes either the way parents would like. Let it be their business, and allow them to experience the consequence of their actions. Parents can set standards for how neat and clean children are to be when they appear in public with adults, but a child as young as five can choose what to wear to school. Mothers who are in the habit of laying out clothes for youngsters are acting like valets. Better to use that time to teach a few lessons to the child in choosing and caring for clothing. At a quiet time, when there is no rush to get ready, show and tell which garments match and go together. Teach about color and suitability so that the child learns what to wear for play and what to wear to school. Demonstrate how to insert a hangar in a garment, or how to fold one that goes into a drawer. Explain that you no longer intend to make the decisions that the child can make, and then allow the youngster to make them. When a youngster is allowed free choice of what to wear, she or he is developing independence in making decisions and is more likely to want also to take care of the clothing appropriately.

Suppose your children are now approaching their teens or are already in their late teens, and you haven't begun any of these procedures? You can still decide to change your method of operation. One of the greatest errors parents make is to continue to hand out money to young adults instead of expecting them to stand on their own two feet. If you continually rescue them from the effects of their poor judgment, they can't learn to have better judgment. They don't learn from their mistakes if someone else is always available to erase the effects of those mistakes. Many parents have discovered that their young adult offspring only learn to cope with the world successfully when their parents stop doing it for them. They may suffer, but they learn to survive.

Money makes many things possible, and the appropriate use of it requires education and experience. Help your children learn to be wise with money while they are with you so that you won't wring your hands with worry when they leave.

chapter eleven

Different Types of Families

Children are all individuals, and the ones we talk about in this book are growing up in families. But families no longer consist of mommy, daddy, and the traditional two plus kiddies. Maybe yours does, and fits the common expectations. If so, you can skip this chapter, for it is written for those adults who live in one of the family variations of today's society. It may consist of two or more adults and one or more children, or the minimum of one parent and one child. Such a single parent may not even be a family all the time, but await the child's periodic visits in order to become one. This may also be true if you are a couple in which one member is the biological parent of a child or children who live most of the time with the other parent. If this is the case, you may be the parent every weekend, or only during school vacations, or at some other time.

Some of the alterations in family makeup are caused by death, some by divorce or separation. Then there are those new combinations or amalgamations formed when children who started out with other parents come to new ones. This happens most often as a result of the remarriage of parents who have been cut off from their previous partners by divorce or death, and who begin a new family life with new partners. This new family may include in addition to children born of other parents, infants born into the new family, the children of both current parents. The children in such a family may include the man's children from an earlier family, now getting acquainted with a woman who will be their maternal parent, or more commonly the woman's children for whom she has custody, now getting acquainted with a new paternal figure. As mentioned above, they may be permanent members of the family or transient visitors.

In this general classification of "other" kinds of families is also the one in which the parents are continuous, but the relationship is not the usual biological one. This would include foster parents whose care is temporary and adoptive parents whose care is permanent and legally authorized. The child, in every case, is in a relationship different from the one he or she was born into.

When a child is adopted as an infant, the differences between the family he or she joins and the family into which a biological child is born are slight. It used to be common for an adopted child not even to know that there was anything different in the situation, but it has been the practice for the past several decades for an adopted child to be informed of her or his origin at a very early age. An additional variation exists in families where there are children born to the parents either before or after a specific child was adopted. Adoption may also solidify the bonds in a combined family. This happens when a father or mother legally adopts the child or children of the other spouse.

A foster child knows the stay in the family is limited,

as do the parents, and this presents unique angles to the relationships. And yet, during the time the child is with the foster family, care must be taken to accept the child into the group and to offer whatever emotional resources are available to support the youngster's development.

Not only children and parents are affected by changed family arrangements, but the extended family as well. In addition to sisters and brothers, there may be grandparents, aunts, uncles, and cousins. All these people can either help or hinder parents and children in creating new chains of affection. Parents cannot control the actions or reactions of any of these other people, nor protect the children from them, but need to be aware of the existence of these other influences on the newly formed group.

However families live together, young children are dependent in them and on the adults and need to grow into independence. Each person in a family has an individual relationship with every other person, whether the family exists on a continuing basis, is disrupted and recreated, or changes in number from time to time. Especially in the case of a new marriage and a new step-parent, that person has to find her or his place in the regard of the child. The biological parent must guard against acting as the go-between, trying to make things be smooth. This applies as well to others in the family, especially siblings. And in the larger circle, new connections will be made between the "new" child and grandparents, relatives, and friends. They may not be exactly as you would hope, but they are not subject to your control. As the parent, you can guard against giving glowing descriptions of one person to another, or by contrast, warning them about each other. Allow everyone to make their own discoveries; they may differ from yours.

It is the differences in relationships among the family members that puzzles parents whose responsibilities toward children are not the usual ones. But the link that connects children and adults in a caring relationship is based on children's dependence. Naturally, the younger the child is when the new family is formed, the greater the child's dependence. A child who is launched into the school years, or older, into adolescence, will already have developed a set of personality traits and habits, as well as a system of beliefs, that probably will accompany him or her through life regardless of the best intentions of the new parent. To realize this is to protect yourself from attempting the impossible. When something about the child is distasteful to you, and you reflect on the parent who may have passed on that trait, remember that that other parent may also be responsible for the things you admire and approve about the child. There is no way to wipe out the effects of the child's earlier experiences. There is only a way to begin today to do what you can to make life fruitful for everybody in the family.

No matter how the family is formed nor what the age of the child or children in it, the common element in the relationship between parents and children is the necessity for the adults to help the children grow from leaning on them to autonomous responsibility. Until the young people are adult there is room for parents to exert an influence, and even with young adults parents carry more weight by what they do or don't do than by what they say.

It might help to notice that in every family, even the so-called "normal" intact families, there are times when a parent is disgusted with the child or children and lays blame on the spouse's upbringing or behavior. But just as children confound us with their unexpected mischief, they are as likely to surprise us with unexpected achievements.

Why, then, make a special point of this "other" type of relationship? Because it is different, parents have an additional set of feelings and concerns toward the children and additional difficulty in knowing how best to act for the welfare of all. One parent may try so hard to be the "perfect" mother or father that the child turns away in order to get out from under the pressure of parental expectations. Another parent may keep such a great distance between himself or herself and the child that both are deprived of the opportunity to enjoy one another and to reap the benefits of the association.

There may be, on the part of either or both parents, a tendency to protect, to cajole, or to woo the child in an effort to strengthen the bond between them. This can happen in any family, but when there is an extra dimension because of the origin of the child or children, the temptation is greater to try harder. Many parents, in their zeal to shape their families to be like all the others, pretend there is no difference. This is in itself an error, for it is impossible to deny reality. The children either know or soon discover their origin, and are usually aware of the disruption that has occurred. To deny it is to bewilder them. No matter what you do or how hard you try, you cannot "make up" to children for what has happened before. There is no way to turn back time, but there are many ways to make the most of every day we live.

There is enough anguish in raising children under any circumstances to make it unnecessary to add more. The family you are faced with may not be the ideal family you had hoped for, but no group ever is ideal anyway. If yours is a different family, beware of trying to ignore the circumstances. Especially if another parent has had an influence on the child who now lives with you, you won't be able to erase that influence. All you can do is form your own bond with the child.

If you try to buy the child's favor with gifts, you'll never know if it is your gifts the child treasures or yourself. If you indulge the youngster's whims in the belief that after suffering so much from the conflict of others he or she deserves to be "spoiled," you will court the unpleasant results of living with a brat. If you maintain a cold distance between yourself and the child who lives with your family either permanently or part-time, you miss out on the possibility of enjoying the child, and vice versa. You may also be issuing one more rejection to a child who more than anything else needs acceptance. You may not be able to fill all the emotional needs for this youngster, and you cannot compensate for the wounds suffered and the scars remaining, but you can remember that healthy independence is a goal for him or her too. Your challenge may be to effect change from a defiant independence, brought on by circumstance, to a friendly one brought about by improved family interaction.

All of the information in the preceding chapters applies to disrupted and rearranged households too. The child in such a situation may need even more than others to become independent and able to direct and control herself or himself. In fostering such development, you may discover that the kind of bond that is forged between you is not exactly what you had hoped for, but it can be as strong as the people involved make it. If you carry an ideal of the perfect family, you are bound to fail to reach it. Discard the ideal and turn your attention to the possible.

If you are in a family in which the origin of the relationships is not the usual biological one, don't attempt to gloss over the differences trying to make your family "just like everybody else's." Use your energies instead to face and accept reality. Do whatever you can to help all of the family members live together in harmony, with maximum opportunity for the enjoyment of one another and maximum opportunity for the development of healthy independence in the children.

There aren't any specific instructions here for what to do in this situation, because anything I would tell you now would only repeat the advice I have given in the earlier chapters. In the last analysis, every child is an individual as is every adult, and the relationship between you will flourish or wither according to how you both behave within it, not according to the child's origin.

chapter twelve

Payoff for Parents

Now that I've told you how to raise your child to be independent, you may be wondering whether it's worth the bother. True, it may be easier to protect your children, to act in such a way that your dependent infants stay that way for the rest of your life. In the face of the likelihood that they will outlive you, how do you expect them to function after you're gone? No matter how long you do live, there may come a time during your lifetime when you and your children are separated by many miles, and you are not readily available for the help they may require.

If you work at it carefully, it is possible to keep them turned to you for everything, as long as you live, and there's no doubt that that can be very gratifying. It always feels good to be needed. It certainly helps one feel important with the thought, "He can't make it without me" or "She asks me about everything. Never makes a move without my advice." Or "I have to be always available to help out."

But beyond that, what have you done to your child? By keeping a youngster dependent on you, you may flatter yourself, but you are crippling the child just as surely as if you broke both her legs and arms too. Broken limbs can heal, but the person who grows into physical adulthood with a broken sense of independence finds it much harder to heal. We value a childlike sense of wonder in adults, and commend the grownup who has kept a child's inquisitive nature, but a person who is grown in body yet childish in emotional stance is not generally one we enjoy or admire. How often have you thought, about an adult you know, "He's acting just like a kid!" Or "She ought to know better than that; That's childish!" And when you had those thoughts, they weren't complimentary or approving, were they?

But the best reason for raising your children to be independent is that it's a lot more fun to be their parent when they are adults. You can then be their friend instead of their protector and enjoy their companionship without worrying what it's going to cost you.

The costs of protecting and defending adult offspring who are dependent on you can be tremendous, both financially and emotionally, as you may know. Among the possibilities are the drain on your monetary resources to help out a young adult whose obligations are greater than the ability to meet them, and the drain on your emotional resources as your adult offspring suffer the sorrow of struggling to get along in the world, encountering heavy difficulties and unable to cope with them.

When, however, you know that the child you raised to adulthood is competent to make decisions and confident of his or her own ability to manage, you are released from a whole complex of worries.

If you try to control your children so that they grow up to fulfill your dreams and ideas, you run many risks. First, they may fail to do so. Another is that they will rebel against you so severely that you lose contact with them. This may happen if they are thrust into sudden independence and realize that they have never learned to be autonomous. This can happen if they go away from home for advanced education or when they take a job. Neither mother nor father can go along in either case. They may look back on their dependence on you and feel angry because you, their parents, did not teach them to be independent.

However, when you enhance their independence while they are young, helping them grow apart from you, you have their continued respect, plus the thrill of watching them unfold and uncover their own possibilities, to form their own ideas and carry them out. There is excitement for you in not knowing how their talents will develop, but it can be the excitement of wonder rather than the excitement of despair. For when they can stand on their own two feet, you don't need to worry about them.

Do you cling to your children, live through them, enjoy their achievements vicariously to give you a sense of worth? If you do, they know it, and regard you with less respect. They save their respect for those people whose lives are full. They want to feel that they can live their own lives, for their own satisfaction, and will gain strength through being responsible for their own errors as well as their own triumphs. If you seek your fulfillment through their lives, you lay upon them the burden for your happiness as well as their own. You are certainly to be pleased at their achievements and bask in any reflected glory, but this is an additional source of satisfaction for you, not your main supply. The heavier burden you may place on your offspring makes it that much harder for them to function. They must then be continually aware of your needs in addition to their own. They can function best when they are free of your demands for performance, when they see that your life has content and meaning for you besides your role as a parent. It works both ways; when you free your children for independence, you get freedom for yourself to live your own life.

There is no such thing as total independence, but the independent person is free to grow, to move, and to act. Every person needs to learn how to deal with the realities of life, and the child who is growing in independence learns this lesson gradually instead of being thrust into awareness suddenly. The parent who is raising that child becomes gradually free to pursue other activities instead of being confronted with emptiness when the grown children leave home.

Consider the benefits of raising your child to be independent. When he or she is as young as three or four, you can rest assured that he will speak up if he needs something when he is away from you. You, the parent, don't need to worry that you're the only one who can meet his needs, the only one who can understand his gestures.

When she or he is five or six, and has been taught how to cross the street to get to kindergarten or to a friend's house, you can depend on his or her ability to get there, to use his or her growing judgment to decide when to step into the street and where to turn the corner for the correct block.

As a child reaches the middle years of exploring, of going away from home, overnight to a friend or longer to camp or visiting, you can trust that he or she knows enough about the world to ask appropriate questions when necessary and to be prudent about encounters with other people.

Then, when adolescence begins, there is likely to be turbulence in the youngster as well as between the teen and the parents, but it will be tempered. Because you have raised an independent youngster, the pressure of peers to do unacceptable acts will not be as effective on your son or daughter. There will always be some social constraints, but the child who is becoming independent is less needy of the approval of others, and in a better position to resist temptations to engage in the use of illegal substances, or to dabble in experimental sex. No parents want their offspring to be carried along by all the expectations of peers, but we are often at a loss to know how to prevent it. One of the side effects of raising a child to be independent is that that child will have the courage to think for himself or herself, to make rational decisions most of the time rather than to go along with the crowd for the sake of being accepted. It is during the years of adolescence that a young person is likely to want to conform to the behavior of others. The dependent one may merely switch from doing what parents want—to doing what the group dictates. The independent one is much more likely to make up his or her own mind.

As your youngsters complete their educations and enter into occupations, you can watch as they expand their own lives. They may surprise you by discovering abilities you never suspected they had, and by going into vocations you never knew. By their discoveries your own awareness is expanded, and richer knowledge, perhaps even additional experiences, become open to you. The daughter whom you had chosen to be a lawyer may amaze you by becoming a civil engineer; the son you expected to become a philosopher may instead become a successful businessman; the one who looked like a budding auto mechanic may become a designer of motors instead, and the one who liked to mix chemicals may become a gourmet cook. There is no end to the possibilities that our children can discover for themselves, if we help them to gain the kind of independence that enables them to see beyond our limits. With the world changing and expanding at its present rate, it is inevitable that opportunities open for our children that we never could imagine.

Similarly, when your daughter or son chooses a mate, you may be surprised, and may even be disappointed in the man or woman presented to you. But if you have the confidence in your own offspring that raising an independent child brings you, you can assume that this young adult is using the same good sense in selecting a mate as she or he has used in other tasks of life up until this time. Even if you don't like, or don't approve of, your new son- or daughter-in-law, or the house mate without marriage, you can accept him or her without restraint. You can trust the judgment of your offspring, knowing that you have done what you can to help them learn and grow.

But the best gain for parents of independent young people is the opportunity to enjoy your middle years, to live your own lives more fully, to have the opportunity to like your children as well as to love them, and to find them interesting companions. Parents who reach such a stage find also that their children are much more likely to seek their company, that family get-togethers are occasions for mutual enjoyment rather than conflict and strain.

If grandchildren arrive, your friendship with your own offspring will pave the way for you to have the fun and frolic with the new little ones that will bring a sense of awe and a new dimension of love and joy to your life. You won't need to feel that you must compensate to the grandchildren for your inadequacy with their parents, nor will you be tempted to lavish them with indulgences so that they will love you. You can be serene in the knowledge that another generation of independent young people is forming.

Although the relationship between the generations remains one of close kinship, it expands to include the best aspects of friendship. Even though most of us in families arrived there by biology rather than by choice, it is possible to bring the period of parental obligation to an end when the children reach adulthood, and thereafter to choose one another as close friends. In that relationship, we can find the best in ourselves as well as in our children, accepting them as human beings of equal value to us, as they accept us as valued people.

chapter thirteen

Directions

Direction means "guidance or supervision of action or conduct" and it also means "the line or course along which something is moving or is aimed to move."

We think of directions in both definitions in the course of our daily lives. We read the instructions for operating an appliance or vehicle, and think about following the directions. Then, as we travel, we think about the direction in which we want to move in order to reach the chosen place.

The foregoing chapters have been directions in the sense of instruction. The following are directions in the sense of a road map. Every time we travel, we have to choose the road, and there is usually more than one path to bring us to our designated destination. In life, too, we have more than one choice in almost every situation, and as parents it is often difficult to decide which way to move. The examples that follow will help you make some of those decisions. The designated destination is independence for your daughter or son, for all your children. The choices you make in how you act, what you say and what you do, influence the development of independence in your offspring. In these situations you can learn for yourself how to direct your children toward independence.

Sheila, ten months old, is crawling around the living room. She approaches the coffee table and starts to creep under it, but it is low, and there is danger that she will bump her head. She moves very slowly, exploring as she goes. Her father is watching. What can he do?

Toward independence: Watch closely as she proceeds, ready to comfort her if she bumps her head and cries. Speak to her so she knows he is near.

Toward dependence: Snatch her away from the table as she approaches it, speaking to her with anger. Scold her for her dangerous act.

Rationale: Sheila is learning about the world. If she bumps her head, the hurt won't do any damage, and she will discover how to protect herself from further hurt as she has the experience and makes the connection between the hurt and the table. As long as someone is there to comfort her when it becomes necessary, she will be moving toward independence combined with caution.

Jordan, seventeen months old, recently learned to walk. He toddles all over the house, investigating everything that looks interesting to him. In the early winter evening, his parents light a fire in the fireplace and Jordan is attracted to it. He wants to go near it to see the flames and feel the warmth increase. His mother works at a desk nearby, watching him. There is a mesh screen in front of the fireplace, free standing. What should his mother do?

Toward independence: Go to the fireplace area, take Jordan by the hand or in her arms; restrain him physically from going nearer. Tell him briefly and calmly about the danger and emphasize that he will not be allowed to go any closer as you hold him while he watches.

Toward dependence: Grab him away from the fireplace area and remove him to his room. Speak to him harshly about being naughty for going too near.

Rationale: Jordan's curiosity is healthy, but the danger is real. He must be protected from harm, but it is important for him to learn as much as he can about the world he lives in. As he grows in understanding and independence, he will recognize danger when he sees it and avoid it.

Rosanne is just past two. She has a sandbox in the back yard, and usually enjoys playing there alone. However, sometimes she tires of it and wanders away, out of the yard towards the sidewalk and the busy street. Her parents want her to learn to play alone, but they don't want her to go where she can get hurt. What can they do?

Toward independence: If there is a gate that can be closed so that Rosanne can't wander away, shut it and lock it. If there is none, recognize that her safety is more important than her freedom, and be ready to restrain her if she goes toward the sidewalk.

Toward dependence: Don't allow Rosanne outside unless a responsible adult is right next to her. Stop her as soon as she moves away from the sandbox.

Rationale: Although it's wise to help Rosanne learn to play alone, this can't be done at the expense of her safety. She does not yet know about the dangers of traffic, and until she learns she must be protected. Her independence can develop within the limits of an adult's vigilance.

Randy is nearly three years old. He runs and falls down often. He seems to be always in a hurry, and it doesn't do any good to tell him to slow down, for he keeps on running. Then he falls, and sometimes his falling makes a loud thump. What needs to be done?

Toward independence: Wait a moment to see if he gets up to go on. If he does not, go to him, help him up and check to see if there is any evidence of the fall—a bump or a cut. If not, release him with a hug and a simple statement such as "Everything's all right. You're fine." If he falls and gets right up to go on, no comment is necessary.

Toward dependence: Run to him at once, pick him up, make a fuss, cuddle him a lot, and speak at length about the need to be more careful. Say something like, "You poor dear, you hurt yourself."

Rationale: Falling down is a normal part of life at this age. Some hurts are less than others. The parent has to make sure the child is all right, but not give a payoff in extra attention. The risk is the child will continue to cry and make a fuss if he knows the parent's response will also be excessive. When he learns that he can survive the occasional bumps and bruises, natural growth and development will make falling down happen less often.

Alben, three-and-a-half, getting ready for nursery school, is trying to dress himself. He takes his pajamas off and puts his underwear on, and then struggles with his T-shirt, finally putting it on backward. He is struggling into his pants when his mother comes in, noticing the T-shirt back to front. Alben doesn't notice; he's concentrating on his legs. What would mother do?

Toward independence: Comment on how well Alben is proceeding, learning to dress himself, saying nothing about the misplaced T-shirt. Be ready to help with shoes if asked for assistance.

Toward dependence: Tell Alben his shirt is on back to front, and insist that he let you take it off and put it on correctly.

Rationale: It is more important for Alben to have a feeling of accomplishment in his increasing ability to do things for himself than that the shirt be on straight.

Ed, four, likes to eat supper with his parents and older brothers and sisters, but his table manners are poor. He prefers to use a spoon instead of a fork, slurps his soup or juice, sometimes leans on the table, and reaches for things inappropriately. When he is corrected he complains that he's doing the best he can. How can his parents maintain decorum under these conditions?

Toward independence: Decrease the expectations of perfection while Ed is learning. At his age, it is enough for him to be making the effort to eat properly without reminders of his shortcomings. Comment on what he does well rather than what he does poorly.

Toward dependence: Separate Ed from the family, treat him like a baby, giving him his meal in advance. Feed him so he can be neat.

Rationale: Ed will learn better manners if he has good models to observe. He will feel more competent managing his own food rather than having it fed to him. The slight annoyance that his lack of manners makes is small compared to his growing independence.

Beth, five, clings to her mother. Although she was reluctant to leave her to go to kindergarten, she now goes regularly and willingly. However, when her friends ask her to come out to play, or to come over to someone else's house, she refuses. She's quite willing to have them come to her house, and tells her mother that she wants to be near her. What can her parent do?

Toward independence: When Beth is invited elsewhere, calmly and quietly take her by the hand, telling her that she's going. Assume that she'll have a good time there and she will. Set a limit on how long she can stay.

Toward dependence: Appreciate Beth's preference, allow her to cling to home and mother and hope she'll outgrow it.

Rationale: Beth may be using the clinging to keep her mother confined and occupied with her. By assuming that she is in fact ready to go to see a friend, her parent can help her believe it, and to make the transition from home to the freedom of the greater world. Setting a time limit will let her know that her parent will be waiting for her to return, giving her the extra assurance she craves.

Carl, eleven, David, nine, and Eileen, six, all go to the same school. In order to be on time, they should be awake by 7:30 A.M. Carl and Eileen usually awaken promptly and begin to get ready, but David habitually oversleeps. He is accustomed to having his mother and/or father come into his room repeatedly to make sure that he gets up and gets started. What can they do to change his pattern?

Toward independence: After discussing the problem at a family meeting, David can be informed that hereafter he will be on his own to get up on time, since he is competent to do so. Neither mother nor father go in to awaken him nor to check on him. He can set his own alarm clock (get one if he doesn't have his own). Let him know that you trust him to get up when it rings and to be responsible for himself.

Toward dependence: Continue as before, possibly enlisting Carl and Eileen for the task of helping to get David up and ready.

Rationale: Under the present system, David has two parents in his service, and the possibility of getting his brother and sister into the act as well. For his own independence, he needs to learn that he *is* capable of taking care of his own regimen, and the only way he can learn is by experiencing the situation. As long as other people are willing to do for him what he could do for himself, he has no incentive to change.

Grace, seven, was at a Brownie meeting after school five blocks from home. The weather turned cold, snowy, slippery. Although she usually walked home from Brownies and had dressed warmly in the morning, her father was worried about how she would make it home.

Toward independence: Wait until the time she would be due to arrive home, and then allow an extra fifteen minutes leeway before going out to see if she needs help.

Toward dependence: Be at the meeting place before Brownies is due to be over, to make sure to take Grace home safely.

Rationale: Since Grace was prepared for the weather and accustomed to walking the distance, she needed to learn she could manage even when the weather changed.

In this particular situation, Grace did make it home alone and came in glowing. She stamped her feet to rid her boots of the snow and said, "I made it! All by myself! You didn't have to come for me!" Her joy was evidence that her parents' decision was correct.

Fred, eight, doesn't do his chores around the house unless he is reminded. Usually, when his mother tells him to take out the garbage or to bring up the clean laundry, he does, but he waits for her to tell him what to do. At a family meeting, he chose those jobs, but he doesn't seem to remember when they are to be done.

Toward independence: Don't remind him, directly or indirectly, after telling him that you no longer intend to do so. He'll learn from whatever consequences ensue.

Toward dependence: Use any method, from timers that ring to charts to be checked, including spoken (or yelled) reminders from either or both parents. That way he'll realize his own incompetence, and feel reinforced at his need to lean on others.

Rationale: Fred is now accustomed to waiting until he is told to do something. He is capable of noticing and remembering when jobs need to be done and will be more apt to pay attention if no one else assumes his responsibility. When he feels and sees the consequences of his failure to perform without reminders he is more likely to take on independent action.

Quinn, ten, and Matthew, eight, brothers, come home from school and go straight to the television set, whether or not they have homework. Their mother says she sometimes greets them at the door to tell them there will be no TV until they finish their work, but in that case they just sit around anyway, complaining they are deprived of their favorite shows. How can this be changed?

Toward independence: Instead of giving orders, the mother might pull the plug on the set, or put it away for a week or a month. She could also assert that the homework is the boys' business and not hers.

Toward dependence: Sit down with them and supervise their homework until it is finished.

Rationale: The homework is the children's responsibility, not the mother's, but the atmosphere in the home is as much hers as anyone else's. The boys may still avoid doing their homework, but changes in the family interaction are certain to follow withdrawal of the television. This can lead to a clearer understanding of respective responsibilities and a thorough discussion at the family council meeting.

Wilma, eight, sets the table for the family meal. As she puts each plate and glass down, she uses extra force so she makes a loud noise with each one. She has been told that she might crack a plate or a glass that way and that the noise is distressing to others, but she still does it.

Toward independence: Just once, tell Wilma that she will have to pay out of her allowance for anything she breaks. Then pay no more attention to the noise.

Toward dependence: Don't let Wilma set the table any more because she doesn't do it correctly.

Rationale: Wilma makes the noise to communicate to someone that she is angry or resentful. She hopes to create a little excitement to get attention. To respond to the noise is to rise to her provocation. To ignore it is to assume that she will quit if she gets no response.

Tom, nine, begged for a dog. He promised that he would take care of it, remember to feed it, and take it for exercise. After weeks of his pleading and assurances, his parents took him to the local humane society where he picked out the dog he wanted. After a few weeks his devotion ebbed and his mother noticed that the dog's water dish was not filled, no food was being offered, and the dog often whined at the door to be taken out. If this situation continues the dog suffers, but if the adults take over, Tom is relieved of responsibility. What can they do?

Toward independence: Tell Tom that you care for the dog when he does not because you will not let the dog suffer because of Tom's neglect. Arrange to return the dog.

Toward dependence: Take care of the dog, making excuses for Tom's neglect, taking over for him so that he can enjoy the dog without any responsibility.

Rationale: The life of the animal is at stake, so you cannot wait for Tom to take care of it, but if he does not fulfill his part of the contract, he cannot continue to enjoy the companionship and ownership of the dog.

Jennifer, eight, is in third grade. As part of an introduction to the life cycle of growing things, her class planted seeds. She brought home a seedling to care for and raise as a plant. She has instructions on care and is to take the plant back to school at the end of the term when she is to make a report and be graded. Since she brought it home, the plant sits on her dresser, unattended. Should someone remind her about it?

Toward independence: The plant is Jennifer's lesson. If she neglects to water it and put it in the light, it will wilt, and she will observe the effects of her neglect. Thus she will learn about her own responsibility.

Toward dependence: Remind Jennifer every day and see that she takes care of the plant so she gets a good mark.

Rationale: If someone reminds Jennifer, she will have no cause to remember. The plant will become someone else's responsibility, and the grade will be due to someone else's thoughtfulness. Even if the plant dies, Jennifer needs to learn that it was hers to take care of, and that it was her neglect that led to its demise.

Kenny, nine, is nearing completion of his second year as a Cub Scout. He says he's bored with it, but continues to go to the meetings at school after classes. He has to decide now whether he will go on with the Scouts next year, into more advanced activity. He shows no enthusiasm, but says he wants to continue. The expense for new uniforms is manageable, but his parents wonder whether he should be allowed to pursue something in which he shows so little interest.

Toward independence: Leave the decision entirely up to Kenny.

Toward dependence: Especially when he can't seem to make up his mind, tell him that you have decided he should quit.

Rationale: This is only one of many decisions with which Kenny will be faced in life. Even if he decides to continue and still doesn't enjoy it, he can't blame anyone else. There may be advantages to being a Scout that he doesn't tell you about, such as being with his friends. By making the decision for him, a parent would deprive him of the opportunity to learn how to make his own.

Tracy, ten, lies around the house for hours. She seems lazy and waits to be prodded before she will study or do any jobs. Her mother and father insist that unless they continue to remind her, sometimes to scream at and threaten her, she never does anything. They don't want to take on her responsibility, but fear that if they don't nag, she won't move. What can they do?

Toward independence: Quit policing Tracy, and allow her to decide what she will do. (She does decide anyway.) Then, when there is harmony in the family, there's at least a possibility that Tracy will learn to take on responsibility. The lazy child is discouraged.

Toward dependence: Continue increasing the pressure.

Rationale: It is highly probable that Tracy's behavior is a rebellion against her parents' demands. She may also be discouraged about her ability to keep up with her studies, to meet the standards set for her, so rather than keep trying, she takes the attitude that it's no use. In order to help her, her parents must remove the pressure and cease to foment conflict and further rebellion. Tracy needs encouragement, not harassment.

Joel, eleven, wants to quit piano lessons. He's been taking weekly lessons for three years, at first with enthusiasm and lately with reluctance. Now he wants to switch to guitar, but there is a piano in the house and no guitar. He rarely practices the piano and then only for twenty minutes after his father nags him for an hour. His parents fear that if he quits the piano now, he'll be sorry later, and they can't buy him a guitar. What can they do?

Toward independence: If Joel wants to quit, there's not much to be gained from trying to force him to continue. Having lost interest, he's not learning. Even though he dutifully goes to his weekly lesson, he has quit learning already.

Toward dependence: Force him to practice or buy him a guitar.

Rationale: To force Joel to continue is to put him in a position where he would be doing it for his parents, not for himself. In buying him a guitar, the parents would be making a sacrifice, probably resenting it, and putting additional burdens of expectation on Joel. In his decision to quit the piano, he is responsible for any later regret. If he really wants to learn to play the guitar, he'll find a way.

Hal, twelve, doesn't stand up straight. No matter how many times he is reminded, he still slumps. He's quite tall for his age and wants to participate in athletics, but his posture is continually poor. His father has offered him a new baseball mitt if he stands up straight for six weeks in a row, followed by a new tennis racket if he stands up straight for another six weeks. Still Hal slumps.

Toward independence: Stop offering rewards, and stop giving reminders. Let Hal decide for himself what kind of posture he'll assume, since he's doing so anyway.

Toward dependence: Continue to remind him, and make the offers more enticing.

Rationale: Only if Hal can develop a good opinion of himself will he feel like standing up straight all the time. If he can know that he is in charge of his own body (as in fact he is), he is much more likely to take command of his spine. By offering him rewards, no matter what they are or how much he wants them, his father leads him to believe that he should stand up straight only for a prize, only to please someone else.

———————

Twins, Ian and John, thirteen, have always shared a room, their clothes, and their activities. Now Ian wants to go off with his friends without John, who is somewhat shy. John would prefer to stay at home and work on his stamps, but their parents feel that Ian should be willing to include John in all his activities, as he has in the past.

Toward independence: Parents stay out of the choices of both boys, so that each of them can develop independently. Even though John is not as outgoing as Ian, if he himself chooses what he wants to do he will be able to develop his own divergent interests.

Toward dependence: Parents could insist that Ian include John, and insist that John accompany Ian. That way they will assure that John remains dependent on other people and less likely to develop autonomy.

Rationale: Even though they are twins, each boy is a separate individual, and needs to develop independence, not just from parents, but from each other.

Vera, fourteen, is in eighth grade and has to decide on her high school curriculum. Her teachers recommend and her parents prefer that she prepare for college, but Vera insists she wants the new cosmetology program. She says she isn't interested in college, but wants to be trained for a job when she graduates. The school personnel require a decision. What can her parents do?

Toward independence: Let Vera decide and take the course of study she wants. If it develops that she is not challenged by the vocational training and wants to go to college, she can learn later how to qualify.

Toward dependence: Tell the school that Vera will enroll in the college preparatory course for which she has the aptitude and intelligence.

Rationale: To force Vera into the program she does not want will only contribute to her resentment and lay the groundwork for retaliation. To allow her to make her own choice will demonstrate your respect for her. If later she decides to try for college, she can. It's more valuable for Vera to learn to make her own decision and live with the consequences than it is for her to do what her parents want.

———

Kathy, fifteen, is a hard worker, and likes to earn money. So far she has a steady clientele for baby sitting, teaches a Sunday school class for which she gets paid, and occasionally tutors younger students for an hourly fee. This results in a great deal of money coming to her regularly while she keeps up her school work and spends time with friends. How can her parents help her learn to manage her money properly and enjoy it too?

Toward independence: If she doesn't already have a savings account, help her to open one. In addition, assist her if necessary to have a checking account for her own use. Teach her how to manage it, and discuss her financial goals with her. Assure her that although the money is hers to control, while she remains financially dependent on you, you will watch how she handles it.

Toward dependence: Require that Kathy turn over all her earnings to her parents, setting aside a fixed amount for her own use. Then parents decide how to handle the money.

Rationale: Since Kathy shows her earning power at an early age, she also needs early lessons in how to handle money. Having her own bank accounts under supervision will help her to learn how to handle her finances when she leaves home in the next few years. At that time she will have had the benefit of her parents' counsel and her own experience.

Pat, fifteen, and Shana, twelve, squabble over the use of the bathroom every night. They both insist on solitary occupancy, even though there is plenty of room. They both keep their tooth brushes and hair blowers in the same bathroom. Pat used to have a monopoly on the late evening hours, but since Shana is older and can stay up later now, she fusses with her hair for a long time, keeping her sister out. There is another bathroom, but neither one will willingly use it. What can their mother do?

Toward independence: Refuse to listen to the demands for intervention and encourage them to work out a system for themselves.

Toward dependence: Stand guard with a clock, allowing a specified time for each one, acting as police.

Rationale: Although the girls' conflict is real, they continue it mainly for the purpose of drawing their mother's attention and service. If the parents ignore the provocation and refuse to try to make peace, the sisters will then have to rely on each other to find a solution. They will be learning how to overcome the actual conflicts of daily life.

Lou, sixteen, wants to go away, several hundred miles, to the regional convention of a youth group to which he belongs. The cost will be around a hundred dollars, and he asks his parents to pay. It is a legitimate group, and his parents are pleased that Lou participates, but a hundred dollars for this purpose is not in their tight budget. The convention is sixty days away.

Toward independence: Tell Lou that he may go if he can earn most of the money before the time he has to pay for the trip. If he has more than half and can show how he will raise the rest at that time, offer to lend it to him for a limited period, to be repaid as he earns more.

Toward dependence: Find or borrow the money, give it to him, and let him go.

Rationale: Lou will value the experience, and his own ability, more if he earns the money himself. When a family lives on a tight budget, it is shielding a young person from reality to try to give money for every valuable opportunity. On the other hand, if Lou shows that he is working hard to earn the money and simply doesn't have enough time to get it all together, it is encouraging to him that you trust him to complete the task and repay the loan.

Ellen, sixteen, just got her driver's license and is legally allowed to drive alone. She interprets this to mean that she can go anywhere in the car if she pays for the gas. Besides the inconvenience to the other drivers in the family who share the one car, her parents are worried about her inexperience. How can they let her drive and still exert some control over where she goes?

Toward independence: Discuss with Ellen the many factors that enter into her use of the car and arrange for a system of graduated limits. Plan together for a short trip first, perhaps a mile or two each way. When she returns on time, extend the distance and the permitted time for the next sojourn. Gradually increasing the length of the trip she may take will allow her to demonstrate her trustworthiness, get more experience, and alleviate her parents' worry.

Toward dependence: Either don't let her drive alone, or let her do whatever she wants, being prepared to rescue her.

Rationale: Only with experience can Ellen learn to be a careful driver. Until she demonstrates that she can be trusted, it is unwise to turn her loose with the car. The risks are great, both to her person and to the automobile, as well as the inconvenience to others in the family. In arranging for her experience to grow in small steps, she will become increasingly capable of sensible independence.

Lance, seventeen, is a high school junior with high test scores and excellent grades. He can probably be accepted in any college, but the trouble is he doesn't know what he wants to study. He thinks he wants to go far away from home, but his parents' moderate income must also provide for younger siblings, and they are reluctant to incur the additional travel and telephone bills that long distance requires. Soon Lance has to narrow his choices so he can visit colleges and prepare applications. What is the parents' role?

Toward independence: Decide the limits of your financial ability and any other requirements you have for his college. These might include distance, type of college (private or public, co-ed or one sex, religious or ethnic makeup, size of student body), academic quality or availability of a wide course selection. Allow Lance to make his own choice from those that meet your criteria.

Toward dependence: Choose for Lance the one you think will be best for him.

Rationale: Although Lance has to decide, his parents will continue to support him, and thus may make certain specifications. In so setting limits, they give him the freedom to make a mutually satisfactory choice. Veto power is unnecessary.

Molly, eighteen, has returned on vacation in her first term at college. She will be at home for three weeks and tosses her soiled clothes into the family wash, assuming that her mother will do the laundry for her as she always did in the past. While she was away at school, Molly did her laundry herself, but on this vacation she brought home two weeks' worth of dirty stuff.

Toward independence: There is no reason for anybody to take on Molly's personal chores. Just as she was capable to do her own laundry at school, she can take care of it at home, acting like a responsible adult.

Toward dependence: Lavish indulgence on Molly now that she's home, taking care of her laundry and any other chores. That way she'll enjoy her vacation more.

Rationale: Molly is en route to adult living, and there is no point in her parents inducing her to behave again like a child. She will have a better sense of her own competence if she learns that she can fend for herself at home as well as away.

Questions parents ask often begin with "What if . . .?" They want to know:

What if the chores don't get done?

What if my child fails in school?

What if the clean kitchen floor gets messy?

What if they don't get to bed on time?

What if the neighbors complain?

What if she really hurts him?

All those doubts are evidence of a pessimistic attitude, a refusal to believe that logical change can make a difference for the better in family life. If you attempt change believing that it won't work, you're already defeated. None of us can answer the "What if?" for we don't have the ability to predict the future. We have to wait and see what happens and then decide how to act next. More important, we have to allow our children to experience the consequences of what happens so they have the opportunity to change.

All beginnings are difficult, and it is certainly hard to begin to change the way you function in your own home. The way to do it is to start with one specific kind of behavior. There is at least one change that will not cause disaster and only you the parent know which one that is.

Keep in mind the child's level of capability. Don't expect a four-year-old to set the table with dishes from a high shelf, nor a six-year-old to remember a list of instructions about getting dinner started. But don't talk down to a ten-year-old who knows very well how to run the vacuum cleaner. Don't underestimate any more than you overestimate them. Help them to reach; acknowledge their growing abilities. Children are not just short people; they are worthy of the same respect we show to adults. Perhaps you need to begin to consider your children in another light: as partners in family life, rather than as dependents who owe you gratitude.

Another question often asked is "How can I change?" Only you can decide to change. A response to that kind of question was recently given by Robert L. Powers, a Chicago psychologist and faculty member of the Alfred Adler Institute, at a session of the Family Education Association in Skokie, Illinois on March 8, 1979. He said, "That's not the question. The question is 'How can you possibly keep on doing what you're doing if it doesn't make sense?' " If you truly see the logic in what I'm saying, and you want to raise your child to be increasingly independent, you will find the way to change.

When you're the navigator on any kind of a journey, you have to figure out where you are before you can know which direction to follow. So it is with raising children. First find out where you are, choose what to do, and watch where you arrive.

Now that you see the possibilities, stop to evaluate where you are. Are you leading your child or children towards independence? Or are you unknowingly following the road toward their continued dependence?

If you were taking a trip on a bus, train, or plane, you'd consult a timetable. Children have their own built-in timetables, and you can't always consult them, so don't worry about the specific time or date, but concentrate on the trip.

Life is movement, and there's always another chance to move in the direction you want to go. There's always some one thing you can do that will help your children become more independent. Choose one at a time, and enjoy the results.

Suggestions for Additional Reading

Adler, Alfred. *The Science of Living*. Garden City, N.Y.: Doubleday Anchor Books, 1969.

Beecher, William and Beecher, Marguerite. *Parents on the Run*. New York: Galahad Books, 1955.

Berman, Eleanor. *The Cooperating Family*. Englewood Cliffs, N.J.: Prentice-Hall, Inc. 1977.

Corsini, Raymond J. and Painter, Genevieve. *The Practical Parent: ABC's of Child Discipline*. New York: Harper & Row, 1975.

Dinkmeyer, Don and McKay, Gary. *Raising a Responsible Child*. New York: Simon and Schuster, 1973.

Dreikurs, Rudolf. *Children: The Challenge*. New York: Hawthorn Books, 1964.

——, Gould, Shirley and Corsini, Raymond J. *Family Council*. Chicago: Henry Regnery, 1974.

Dunn, Rita and Dunn, Kenneth. *How to Raise Independent and Professionally Successful Daughters*. Englewood Cliffs, N. J.: Prentice-Hall, 1977.

Gordon, Thomas. *Parent Effectiveness Training*. New York: Peter H. Wyden, Inc. 1970.

Gould, Shirley. *Teenagers: The Continuing Challenge:* New York: Hawthorn Books, 1977.

——, *The Challenge of Achievement: Helping Your Child Succeed*. New York: Hawthorn Books, 1978.

Mayer, Greta and Hoover, Mary. *Learning to Love and Let Go*. New York: Child Study Association, 1965.

Weinstein, Grace W. *Children and Money*. New York: Charterhouse, 1975.

Index